Kit   Ludo.

106 mins	20ml.	66 mins	140 ml.
92.	210.	75.	280
88	210	57	320
49.	400	61.	190.
66	320	155	260
53.	260	54	360
96	185.	73	170.
340	1605	541	1720
4 4		4	

The
TARKA TRAIL
A Walkers' Guide

540mins. 1,605ml.   541mins. 1,720ml.

The TARKA TRAIL
A Walkers' Guide

With a description of the route by
Richard Williamson

Produced by the Tarka Project

DEVON BOOKS

First published in Great Britain by Devon Books 1992
Reprinted 1993, 1995, 1997 and 1998

British Library Cataloguing in Publication Data

The CIP Record for this publication is available from the British Library

ISBN 0 86114 877 0

DEVON BOOKS
Official Publisher to Devon County Council

Halsgrove House
Lower Moor Way
Tiverton EX16 6SS
Tel: 01884 243242
Fax: 01884 243325
www.halsgove.com

This book was originally funded and produced on behalf of the Environment and Countryside Committee of Devon County Council. The County Environment Director is Edward Chorlton. The book was written and maps originated by the Tarka Project, a Devon County Council initiative in partnership with the Countryside Commission, Mid, West, Torridge and North Devon District Councils.

Printed and bound by BPC Wheaton Ltd., Exeter

CONTENTS

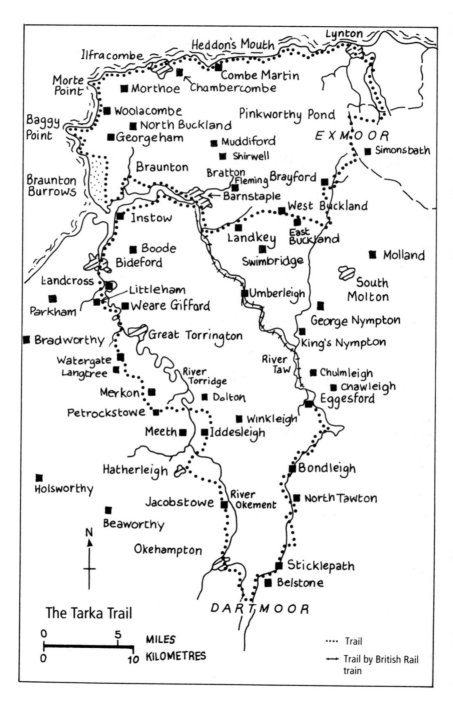

Lynton

Heddon's Mouth

Ilfracombe

Combe Martin

Morte Point

Morthoe

Chambercombe

Baggy Point

Woolacombe

Pinkworthy Pond

North Buckland

Georgeham

EXMOOR

Braunton

Muddiford

Simonsbath

Shirwell

Braunton Burrows

Bratton Fleming

Brayford

Barnstaple

West Buckland

Instow

Landkey

East Buckland

Boode

Swimbridge

Molland

Bideford

South Molton

Landcross

Umberleigh

Littleham

Parkham

Weare Gifford

George Nympton

Bradworthy

Great Torrington

King's Nympton

Watergate

River Taw

Langtree

River Torridge

Chulmleigh

Merton

Dolton

Chawleigh

Petrockstowe

Eggesford

Meeth

Winkleigh

Iddesleigh

Hatherleigh

Bondleigh

Holsworthy

North Tawton

Jacobstowe

River Okement

Beaworthy

N

Okehampton

Sticklepath

Belstone

The Tarka Trail

DARTMOOR

0   5   MILES
0   10 KILOMETRES

···· Trail

⟶ Trail by British Rail train

HOW TO USE THIS GUIDE

The entire 180-mile Tarka Trail is described in this guide, which has been designed primarily for the long-distance walker, although it will be of value to anyone interested in walking the route. The guide is in two parts:

1. **General Introduction,** including advice to walkers, safety and equipment.
2. **The Route,** which is described in 9 sections, with maps opposite each route description. Each of these sections also includes a description of the area by Richard Williamson, the son of Henry Williamson author of *Tarka the Otter.*

The maps and route descriptions in this guide, accompanied by Ordnance Survey maps, should be sufficient for walkers to find their way. The route is also waymarked as an aid to this guide, with a stylised otter paw print in the centre of an arrow. **Following the waymarks without the guide will not allow you to follow the route as the waymarking is designed to be low key and non-obtrusive.**

The colour of the waymark denotes the status of the path you are on as follows:

Yellow – Public footpath
Blue   – Public bridleway
Black   – County road
Green – Permissive path

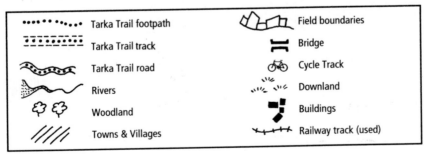

Along the coast path the route is waymarked by the National Trail acorn logo, and within Exmoor National Park the otter paw print has been incorporated into the existing wooden signs. In Dartmoor National Park there are no waymarkers at all, to preserve the naturalness of the moor.

Key to Maps

••••••••••	Tarka Trail footpath		Field boundaries
‑‑‑‑‑‑‑‑‑‑	Tarka Trail track		Bridge
	Tarka Trail road		Cycle Track
	Rivers		Downland
	Woodland		Buildings
/////	Towns & Villages	⁺⁺⁺⁺⁺	Railway track (used)

The maps are drawn approximately 2 inches to the mile.

River Torridge, near Dolton

PART ONE

General Introduction

THE

TARKA TRAIL

The Tarka Trail is a long-distance footpath enabling quiet exploration of the North Devon countryside as described by Henry Williamson in his classic *Tarka the Otter*.

The 180 mile route forms a large figure-of-eight circuit centering on Barnstaple. The southern loop follows a former railway line from Barnstaple to Bideford around the shore of the Taw/Torridge estuary, before heading inland along the Torridge valley. It passes through the heart of rural Devon to Okehampton, crosses part of north Dartmoor and then follows the River Taw from its source back to the estuary and Barnstaple (the last 32 km – 20 miles – being a train journey on the Tarka Line from Eggesford). The northern loop leaves Barnstaple through rolling countryside to the open grass and heather moorland of Exmoor. From here it follows the river valleys down to Lynmouth, and then the dramatic cliff coastline westwards via Ilfracombe and Braunton before reaching the Taw/Torridge estuary and returning to Barnstaple.

The Trail follows a former railway line (parts of which are open to cyclists and horse riders), rights of way (footpaths, bridleways, tracks and occasionally minor roads), and at times permissive paths, which have been created with the kind permission of the landowner. Much of the time the route crosses private land and it is important for walkers to keep to the path and follow the Country Code to help us to maintain the goodwill of the landowners. The route also passes through both Dartmoor and Exmoor National Parks, National Trust land, a National Nature Reserve, and Forestry Commission land. Please keep dogs under strict control at all times, but in particular across farmers' fields, along riverbanks and in open moorland in the lambing season.

Safety and Equipment

The Trail passes through a variety of landscapes and ranges from very gentle walking on the former railway line to the rigours of open moorland and steep climbs on the coast path. It is essential to wear appropriate footwear and to ensure you have good waterproofs and spare clothing. Even in summer the weather can be unpredictable and on the moorland sections, where mist can rapidly descend, a compass along with the appropriate Ordnance Survey sheet, is vital. There are also some parts of the coast path where a map and compass should be carried in case of poor visibility. Walkers should also carry a whistle on the moors and be aware of the international distress signal – six long blasts.

When on the former railway line, please respect other users. Walkers be aware that cyclists may come up silently behind you. Cyclists and horse riders slow down to walking pace and make sure walkers are aware of your presence before attempting to pass or overtake.

The Trail crosses many rivers and streams and at times follows riverbanks. Care needs to be taken in these areas as currents can be fast and the water much deeper than it appears. Water levels can also rise very rapidly following heavy rain, particularly on and around the moors.

Whenever the route follows a road, walkers should face oncoming traffic by keeping to the right-hand side.

Planning your route

The Trail is an ideal two week walk, if you cover an average of about 16km (10 miles) a day, It is advisable to book your accommodation in advance, particularly in the summer season. Tourist Information Centres are valuable sources of accommodation information, and can direct you to other places of interest along the way. It is possible to reach the start point at Barnstaple by British Rail train, and with the new link road (A361) to Barnstaple and improved A30 to Okehampton, driving to the area is very easy. Also remember the last 32km (20 miles) are by British Rail train so find out train times when you plan.

Those walkers wishing to make the trip across north Dartmoor to Cranmere Pool should check the Ministry of Defence range notices for firing times in the relevant ranges. These are available at the Tourist Information Centre and Police Station in Okehampton and are printed in the Friday edition of the *Western Morning News*.

The guide should provide sufficient information to follow the route, but it is advisable to carry the 1:50 000 Ordnance Survey sheets 180 and 191 to give wider information. For sections on Dartmoor and Exmoor 1:25 000 maps should be carried (Outdoor Leisure sheet 28 or Pathfinder Series SX 49/59 and SX 69/79 for Dartmoor and SS 64/74 for Exmoor). The set of thirteen 1:25 000 maps will give even greater information for walkers (SS 42/52; SS 41/51; SS 40/50; SX 49/59; SX 69/79; SS 60/70; SS 61/71; SS 62/72; SS 43/53; SS 63/73/ SS 64/74; SS 44/54; SX 69/79).

Before setting out

To make the most of walking the Tarka Trail, *Tarka the Otter* is ideal background reading. It describes the area in depth and much remains unchanged since Henry Williamson's day, the 1920s.

Do not expect to see otters. They still live in the 'Country of the Two Rivers', but are elusive and largely nocturnal animals. They are already under great pressure from pollution and the destruction of their habitat, so please take very special care not to cause them additional disturbance. Please keep to the paths, keep away from riverbanks, and keep dogs under strict control, preferably on a lead. If you would like to see otters, perhaps the best way is to visit the Tamar Otter Park run by the Otter Trust at Navarino, North Petherwin, near Launceston. The Trust is a registered charity which exists to promote the conservation of otters throughout the world. The Park is about an hour's drive from Barnstaple. Asian otters, which are close relatives of European otters, can be seen very close to the Trail, at the Combe Martin Wildlife Park.

Always be aware when you are in the countryside, particularly of the wildlife that surrounds you, and remember that people live and work here. Please remember to follow the Country Code:

- Enjoy the countryside and respect its life and work
- Guard against all risk of fire
- Fasten all gates
- Keep your dog under close control
- Keep to public paths across farmland
- Use gates and stiles to cross fences, hedges and walls
- Leave livestock, crops and machinery alone
- Take your litter home
- Help to keep all water clean
- Protect wildlife, plants and trees

POLLUTION HOTLINE – If you see pollution, please ring the NRA (National Rivers Authority) – free – on their 24-hour emergency number: 0800 378500.

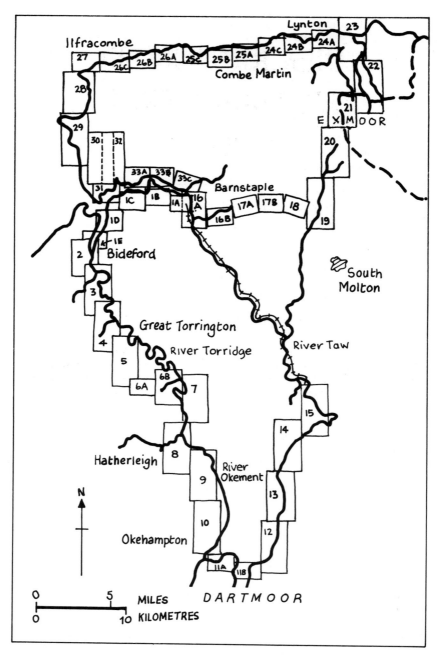

Tarka Trail route showing individual map sections.

4

PART TWO

DESCRIPTION OF THE TARKA TRAIL ROUTE

This section includes text written by Richard Williamson and a route description (adjacent to the maps) for each of the nine sections.

PLEASE NOTE: Many of the places mentioned in Richard Williamson's text are on private land. The only access is along the Tarka Trail, or on other public rights of way. Please respect the landowners and do not stray from the path.

AN INTRODUCTION TO TARKA COUNTRY

My father, Henry Williamson wrote *Tarka The Otter* at Georgeham, Devon in the 1920s. The book was first published in 1927 and was awarded the Hawthornden Prize for Literature the following year. Since that time it has never been out of print, has been translated into many languages, and still has thousands of copies printed every year.

The countryside of North Devon with its wild moorland, rocky coast, tumbling rivers and deep wooded valleys was paradise to him after the London suburbs and First World War battlefields which was all he had ever known before. For many, this countryside offers exactly the same refuge from the horrors of modern life today, for it has not changed very much since the writing of *Tarka*. You can see the same woods and meadows, moors and rivers, bridges, villages and rocky headlands. What has changed is that some river-life, including the population of otters, has declined due to pollution. But by following this trail you can understand more about the pressures on this delicate habitat and help towards a solution. You will follow Tarka's route as imagined by my father, who walked everywhere, on many occasions, in winter and summer to get every fact correct. Often he went out with the Cheriton Otter Hounds, watching every move of both hunters and hunted. It was during these excursions that he met his future wife, my mother, whom he married in 1925.

He called the area 'The Country of the Two Rivers' and Tarka's story 'His Joyful Water Life'. The origin of the name Tarka is obscure. HW said that he made it up, but later discovered that it was actually a Celtic word meaning 'little water wanderer' or 'wandering as water'. He did not find it an easy book to write and it was

5

rewritten and corrected many times. It was originally called *An Otter's Saga* and then abandoned with a diary note despairing that it was any good or had any purpose in literature. The manuscript was shown to otter hunters, some of whom were dismissive but one, the hunt master, W.H. Rogers was constructive and kindly and so received the dedication, whilst Lord Fortescue of the neighbouring estate of Castle Hill, himself an established writer of country books, wrote the Foreword. Amongst others who gave it serious consideration was Lawrence of Arabia, who described Chapter 9 (The Great Winter) as amongst the finest writing in the English language.

The Tarka Trail itself makes a figure-of eight with Barnstaple as its pivot. Because of its central position and travel facilities it is convenient to make Barnstaple the starting and ending point but, as readers of the book will know, the actual story begins and ends at Canal Bridge on the River Torridge near Torrington. The Trail follows paths and old railway lines, minor roads and coastal footpaths, crosses meadows and moors. It is never far from the sound and movement of water. It is waymarked for convenience but for much of the way it crosses private farmland and visitors should walk with care and consideration for domestic animals as well as wildlife and other users, leaving no litter and closing gates, and not disturbing nesting birds (which is actually illegal).

You don't have to explore the whole Trail on foot. Only the keenest walkers amongst you will probably do the full 180 miles. It is possible to hire bicycles for the railway sections of the trail and this is an excellent way to travel. Or you can use buses to get the major points and then explore shorter distances on foot. The railway too, with its Tarka Line from Exeter to Barnstaple affords good views of the whole of the Taw valley. Stop off at intermediate stations and explore those landmarks vital to the Tarka story. There is also much of interest throughout the area that is not directly connected with the actual Tarka Trail and the Tarka story, so do take the opportunity to widen your horizons.

The Tarka Trail is, however, the visible centrepiece of Devon County Council's work to promote conservation, tourism and recreation in North Devon. Named 'The Tarka Project' it aims to care for and improve wildlife, to conserve the famous Devon landscape, and to help interpret this for the visitor and to ensure that this special part of England remains in a fit state to hand on to future generations. It is a magical place to explore both in the pages of the book and along this trail laid out for you now. *Tarka the Otter* (from which quotes appear throughout this book) is a classic of English literature. It is a work of vivid imagination but it was so rooted in the reality of the Devon landscape that you too can walk nearly every part of the way that Tarka took, and see all the scenes that HW described so many years ago.

Richard Williamson

SECTION 1 TAW/TORRIDGE ESTUARY

With the ebb Tarka drifted, slowly and unseen, floating by ketches and gravel barges, while ring-plover and little stints running at the line of lapse, cried their sweet cries of comradeship. The mooring keg bobbed and turned in the ebb; the perches tattered with seaweed leaned out of the trickling mud of the fairway, where curlews walked sucking up worms in their long bills. Tarka rode on with the tide. It took him into the estuary, where the real sea was fretting the sandbanks.

The meeting of fresh and saltwater achieves spectacular results in the estuary of the Taw and Torridge. Twice daily the head of fresh water carried by both rivers from their sources on Dartmoor is let go and each winds stealthily out to sea through the 'channers' and 'guts' of the saltmarsh and sandbanks. But within six hours the Atlantic Ocean returns, forcing its own glittering spears of water into the heart of the landscape, running up to Barnstaple and on beyond the town, and in the south to Bideford and on up through the enclosing hills for a mile. It is a landscape well known to millions of tourists taking the road along the coast to Braunton and Croyde and to Bideford on the southern side of the estuary. It will be a nostalgic memory for many who once used the passenger railway service, hauled by semi-streamlined Merchant Navy Class locomotives in their livery of spring green, axed in the Beeching cuts of the 1960s. The line running from Barnstaple included the famous ascent back out of Ilfracombe, the second steepest in Britain. Today the Tarka Trail follows the old railway line from Barnstaple to Bideford, and also back to Braunton on the other side of the estuary.

It was to these saltwaters of the estuary that Tarka was forced to retreat in the 'Great Winter' scene when he and his mate caught a wild swan. It was here too that he saw the old grey Jaark. Estuary birds are still found here, sometimes in great flocks. Wild duck, such as wigeon, teal and mallard seek shelter here from the harder frosts of eastern Britain. Flocks of small wading birds, turning like shoals of fish in the sun, fly here from breeding grounds in the Arctic. Dunlin, curlew, redshank, oystercatcher are among a dozen species that use the estuary all winter, feeding on ragworm, cockles, limpets, sandhoppers, and a huge variety of other sea animals. Many roost at high tide on the RSPB's reserve at Isley Marsh, an area of saltmarsh near the old coal-fired power station (now dismantled). Summer visitors will not see birds in such great numbers but should have good glimpses of ringed plovers, oystercatcher, redshank and turnstone. It is the wildfowl which contribute to the designation of the estuaries and their shoreline as a Site of Special Scientific Interest, along with plants like sea lavender, sea purslane, seablite and glasswort.

The estuaries have, during Britain's developing history as a maritime nation over four hundred years, with the shipyards at Appledore, contributed a great deal to the production of sailing ships; a replica *Mayflower* was constructed here in the 1970s and sailed to America. Sailing still flourishes at the attractive little town of Instow.

The fine stone quay and long bridge at Bideford are reminders of the past history of trading by ship to many parts of the country and Europe. Because of the dangerous nature of the bar, where the fresh waters merge finally with the ocean, twenty ships foundered between the years 1627 and 1908.

Tarka travels this way more than once in his journeys. The first time he passes under Bideford bridge is evocatively described as he narrowly escapes the burning ashes thrown out of a house window at Instow. It is in 'the seagoing waters' of the Torridge that we last see him, as the tide turns at that fateful moment.

MAPS AND ROUTE DETAILS

SECTION 1 TAW/TORRIDGE ESTUARY BARNSTAPLE TO BIDEFORD

15 kilometres (9 miles)

MAPS 1A, B, C, D

From Barnstaple the Tarka Trail follows the former railway line managed by Devon County Council's Countryside Management Service.

Turn left out of the railway station, through the car park and follow the country park signs under the road bridge on to the cycleway. This takes you along the shores of the estuary of the rivers Taw and Torridge past Fremington Pill, the RSPB reserve at Isley Marsh and on to Instow. (For village services turn right on to the road as you reach the signal box). Cross the road to the renovated signal box (open to visitors on Sundays during the summer), and carry on alongside the estuary for another three miles to Bideford. The Trail goes past Bideford Station, which now houses the Countryside Management Service Offices. Bideford town is across the 'long bridge'.

MAP 1 A

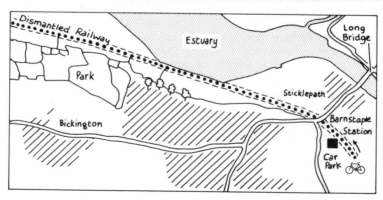

Section 1: Taw/Torridge Estuary

MAP 1 B and C

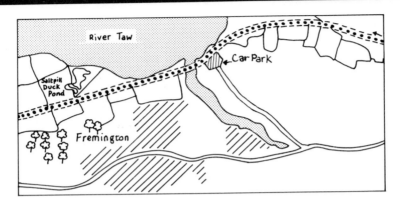

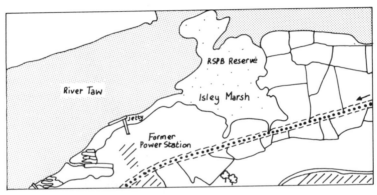

Section 1: Taw/Torridge Estuary

Barnstaple Long Bridge

MAP 1 D

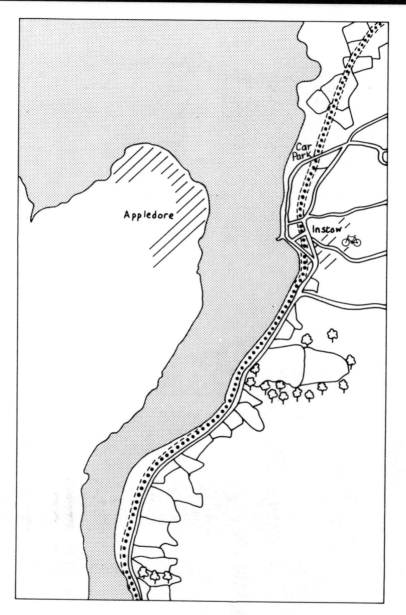

Section 1: Taw/Torridge Estuary, Instow

MAP 1 E

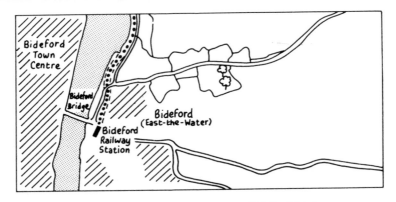

Section 1: Taw/Torridge Estuary, Bideford Station

Bideford Signal Box

SECTION 2 RIVER TORRIDGE

The river flowed slowly through the pool, a-glimmer with the clear western sky. At the tail of the pool it quickened smoothly into paws of water, with star-streaming claws. The water murmured against the stones. Jets and rills ran fast and shallow to an island, on which grew a leaning willow tree. Down from here the river moved swift and polished. Alder and sallow grew on its banks. Round a bend it hastened, musical over many stretches of shillet.

. . . Time flowed with the sunlight of the still green place . . . the otters hunted and ragrowstered for many days under the high wooded hills below which the river wound and coiled like a serpent.

These words were written in the early 1920s but this is still the scene that you will see all around you today. Here the river Torridge is still part of the tidal flow, and the banks are soft silt and shiny at ebb. Above Bideford, Landcross hamlet was the home of HW's bride, and the couple were married in its tiny church on 5 May 1925. The author therefore spent much time here when writing Tarka and at Canal Bridge planned the book.

Now a private driveway, the bridge was an aqueduct and at one time did carry a canal; it gives a splendid view of the river far below, with occasional glimpses of salmon and trout but more likely those of grey mullet in summertime, moving in small shoals up to their breeding grounds. Tarka's birthplace was a riverside holt below the bridge, and although the original twelve trees that HW describes in his opening scene were destroyed some years ago, twelve more oaks and ash have been planted. Tarka was born here and here he also dies, or 'was seen no more'. And here it was, with poignant coincident, on 13 August 1977 that the death scene of Tarka was filmed (for the David Cobham/Rank film) on that very same day HW himself died.

If there is anywhere in England that otters are likely still to be seen it is on this river and others like it in North Devon. However, the chances of seeing the live animal are rare. Firstly they are shy and wary, and tend to be nocturnal, with dusk and dawn as favoured travelling times. Secondly, for much of its journey through the water it moves beneath the surface, hunting fish and hidden from humans. Only a line of bubbles marks its passing as it breathes slowly out and as air bubbles leave the coat. It may be able to stay underwater for up to ten minutes according to the otter hunters of yore and it will generally surface under a bank to breathe.

More likely to be seen are the spraints (droppings) placed on special stones to help mark their territory. These are blackish and shiny and may show the scales and bones of fish. The seals (footprints) are distinctive too, being five-toed but without showing the claws as does a badger. A dog's tracks are four-toed. Otters may travel around a territory that might reach for twenty miles. They have young at any time of the year and the young are born blind and helpless and are not able to swim for a month. The breeding place is called a holt and sometimes is only reached beneath water through a hidden entrance.

At Beam Weir salmon are sometimes to be seen leaping upwards through white water, and it was here that Old Nog, the heron characterised in the book, became greatly excited at the sight of so many elvers crawling over the edge of the weir during migration. According to old records Beam Weir was notorious amongst the hunters for losing otters who would hide in hollows inside the weir: these hollows were considered 'impregnable' but could be made to release their occupants with 'judicious doctoring' – whatever that might have meant.

MAPS AND ROUTE DETAILS

SECTION 2 RIVER TORRIDGE BIDEFORD TO WATERGATE

11 kilometres (7 miles)

MAPS 2 + 3

About a mile after leaving Bideford Station you cross Landcross Viaduct, or 'Iron Bridge' as it is called locally, over the River Torridge. The next four miles to Torrington take you along the Torridge valley, passing Halfpenny Bridge at Annery Kiln, the village of Weare Giffard, and across the river near Canal Bridge and again above Beam Weir. Torrington Station, now a pub called 'The Puffing Billy' is on the outskirts of Torrington, which is less than a mile across the commons or along the main road. After leaving 'The Puffing Billy' the Trail again crosses the river Torridge over a viaduct from which you can see Rothern Bridge just downstream of the road bridge. The path soon runs alongside Langtree Lake, the stream which Tarka and his family followed from the Torridge to Merton Moors, to the car park at Watergate Bridge.

Canal Bridge near Weare Giffard

13

MAP 2

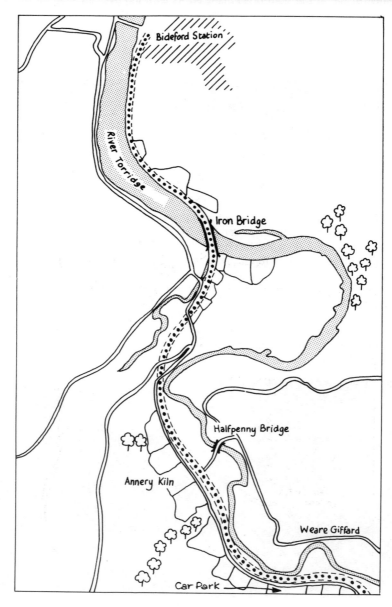

Section 2: River Torridge, Bideford to Weare Giffard

MAP 3

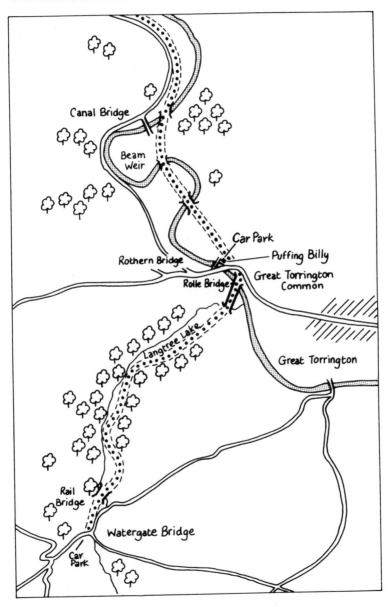

Canal Bridge

Beam Weir

Rothern Bridge

Car Park

Puffing Billy

Rolle Bridge

Great Torrington Common

Langtree Lake

Great Torrington

Rail Bridge

Watergate Bridge

Car Park

Section 2: River Torridge, Weare Giffard to Watergate Bridge

15

SECTION 3 CLAY COUNTRY

They crossed the railway track near a tall dark chimney that rose out of buildings and came to a deep reed-fringed pond ... The pond was an old pit from which white clay had been dug. Round the edge grew reed-maces. Mother and cubs roved about in the water for a while and were joined by an old dog otter whose wandering years being over now dwelled among the reeds and rushes of the White Clay Pits ... His great joy was to play in and out of a rusted, weed grown engine that had lain for years half-buried in the clayey ooze. For three years he had lived on the frogs and eels and wildfowl of the ponds. The clay-diggers often saw him as they went home in the trucks, they called him Marland Jimmy.

Before leaving Torrington, which towers high above the Tarka Trail on its fortress-like hilltop, it is well worthwhile to digress into the town to find the vantage point where the old castle stands. For it is here that the Torridge can be seen at its best. A wooded cliff falls three hundred feet below the town where in sunlight the river's mile-long arc curves displaying its million movements over stones like Arabian silver filigree. On the south-eastern outskirts of the town are the Town Mills where Tarka hid in the wheel and where he was so precipitously thrown down when the millers resumed work after their lunch break. Today the mill has been renovated into holiday flats, but it is possible to lean over the bridge and recapture the age-old atmosphere (but beware the horrendous traffic which barely slows for the right-angled bridge structure). Just a little further up the river is Dark Hams Weir where Tarka rests before the final phase of the last hunt.

To return to the Trail itself; oak and ash, birch, sallow, alder and hazel line the walk as it climbs along the old railway line, originally the Marland Light Railway conceived in 1831, that until the 1980s carried clay from the pits higher up. The walking is easy, the scenery superb. The little stream sings its way downwards besides the track, wandering from side to side, with as many notes as Pan-pipes. Watergate Bridge provides a sturdy parapet on which to lean and rest, to watch the water, to mark, learn and digest. Then on, gently upwards.

In summertime tall wildflowers line the way of the walk; meadowsweet, hemp agrimony and hardhead, flowers that attract many hoverflies and butterflies for nectar. Hart's-tongue ferns hang from the rocks, lapping water that trickles out of the hilly meadows. Buzzards and crows soar through the narrow ravines which, with their spruce and larch plantations climbing steeply upwards, sometimes resemble Austrian hill country.

Eventually the path comes on to Merton Moor. Some of the old moorland plants remain such as bell heather, lesser gorse (flowering in autumn) and fleabane. A soft white tacky clay was deposited here thousands of years ago, and in the past one hundred years has been mined, forming shallow swampy lakes and ponds. It is the haunt of wild duck and moorhen, hidden by sallow willows and scrubby oaks. It was always a favourite place for otters and probably still is today. Otter hunters of the 1900s recorded how difficult it was to follow the hounds, heavier members 'sinking into the clayey ooze'. The rusty pipe in which the friendly old dog otter, Marland Jimmy, loved to play was the funnel of a steam engine which had actually sunk there sometime at the beginning of the century.

16

SECTION 3 CLAY COUNTRY WATERGATE
TO PETROCKSTOWE
11 kilometres (7 miles)

MAPS 4 + 5

Along this section of the Trail you pass many of the places that Tarka and his family visited, including the claypits where they met and played with Marland Jimmy. Take care crossing the road at Yarde as clay lorries drive along here.

MAP 4

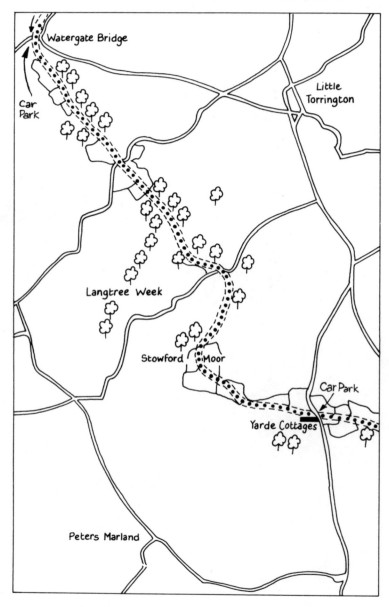

Watergate Bridge

Little
Torrington

Car
Park

Langtree Week

Stowford Moor

Car Park

Yarde Cottages

Peters Marland

Section 3: Clay Country, Watergate to Yarde

MAP 5

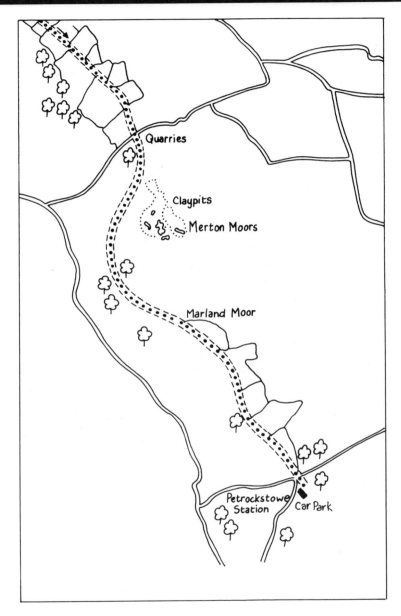

Section 3: Clay Country, Yarde to Petrockstowe

SECTION 4 RIVER OKEMENT AND DARTMOOR

Bogs and hummocks of the Great Kneeset were dimmed and occluded; the hill was higher than the clouds ... Broken humps, rounded with grey moss and standing out of the maze of channers, made the southern crest of the hill. In the main channer, below banks of crumbling peat, lay water darkstained and almost stagnant. Tarka ran past a heap of turves, set around the base of a post marking Cranmere Tarn, now empty, whither his ancestors had wandered for thousands of years.

HW does not detail how Tarka gets to Dartmoor. Chapter 11 opens with him already there as in the passage quoted above. But he would have wandered along much as the Tarka Trail does, using the Torridge and the Okement and their inter-connecting rills and meadows, and clambering over the black rocky shillets in which tough little brown trout dart and hide as in mountain streams.

The farmland that you will cross was once moorland itself and its far views of the great moor, its rolling green distances and scattered sheep flocks are reminiscent of the still half-wild landscapes of Spain and Portugal. Bracken, soft rush and gorse are all too ready to start a return to moorland; the hedgerow beeches on hills lean from fierce winter gales. There are woods still with the 1920s names, such as Braund's Hill wood in which during an earlier adventure Tarka's sister was caught in a gin trap and then shot by a keeper. Now a plantation, there are still hazel shrubs inside the wood as mentioned in the book, when the otters frightened a gang of stoats, or vairs, from beneath a pile of thatching faggots.

Hatherleigh 'village' (more, market town) hangs on the side of a hill, its steep winding roads hemmed even more narrowly by thatched inns: 'The George' was part of Tavistock Abbey estate until the Dissolution of the Monasteries. It still seems part of it. Monks were renowned for their food and hospitality. The present owners need not fear their disapproval. Before the age of the car and lorry the winding streets must have proved even more difficult for the horse.

Rivers, streams and brooks drain the hills. Hatherleigh Moor with its Cleopatra monument to a Balaclava victim looks across to the blue outline of the higher, sterner moor seven miles away. Sometimes the lanes stream with water between high banks. Just before Okehampton the sound of the river comes up through the trees, for the Okement foams in tumbling leaps over waterfalls and slides. The water is glassy, it glissades in clear arcs and the dipper sings in the darkness of deep shade and wades into and under its speckled white foam.

Okehampton – a fragment of metropolis with high-street shops and a superb remnant of Victorian industrial design in the little alley which houses a most interesting museum, full of local background information – ends abruptly at the moor where cattle-grids mark a different world.

The Trail approaches the wildest part of Devon, perhaps of England, for there is nothing else so forsaken, so inhospitable or dangerous as the heights of Dartmoor.

It was to the wilderness that Tarka made his Odyssey after the death of his mate Greymuzzle. He travelled this land of swirling mist and sphagnum bogs where Bronze Age man once lived in stone and peat hutments, while stone circles of their lost religion remain there to this day.

Dartmoor is strewn with granite tors, the word meaning 'tower' derived from the celt *Twr*. There are as well many clatters, or clitters, which are the strewn and shattered remnants of ruined tors. There are hut circles and stone rows and circles, the latter sometimes associated with burial chambers, or 'cists'. Much of the peat has been fissured and hollowed, some of these containing 'featherbeds' or 'quakers', hiding a bog of black ooze beneath an inviting green covering of moss. Mires of swamps are the sodden sponges of peat that form at the head of streams, and ponies have been known to be fatally stuck therein, a fate that might possibly befall an unwary human. The local term for being trapped is 'sugged'.

The intrepid among you will not be able to resist making the pilgrimage to Cranmere Pool. In fine weather it is not at all difficult, but it is well to be prepared for all eventualities (including compass, whistle, wet-weather gear and emergency rations).

At least five rivers begin near Cranmere Pool, fed by Atlantic rains, including both Torridge and Taw. Long ago it was a deep, wet area with reeds and a strong enough head of water to give each progeny a lusty cry as it began life to flow east, south, west, or north. In 1844 the tarn was breached and the pool drained away but fascination for this 'mother of rivers' remained and for Victorians it became a romantic challenge of navigation and daring. Charles Dickens and in 1921, the late Duke of Windsor as Prince of Wales, were among eminent people to make the pilgrimage and leave visiting cards in a special bottle hidden in a cairn. A visitors' book now held in the Local Studies department of Plymouth City Library records that HW came here in 1926, gaining his impressions for Tarka's journey.

Today, you can have your letters stamped with the special Cranmere Pool postmark. While it is perhaps not so wild as it used to be it is well worthwhile accepting the challenge in order to savour the very special atmosphere of wilderness still engendered here.

MAPS AND ROUTE DETAILS

SECTION 4 RIVER OKEMENT AND DARTMOOR
PETROCKSTOWE TO OKEHAMPTON
34 kilometres (21 miles)

MAP 6A + 6B

After leaving Petrockstowe Station, continue on the railway line for approximately 2 km (1 ¼ miles) and then turn left, over the stile into the fields. The Trail now heads north-east for about 4km (2½ miles). Follow the waymarked permissive path to Bourna Farm. At the road go over the stile and turn left, crossing the road after a short distance opposite the next stile and continue following the waymarks till you meet the road again at Broadmead crossroads, turn right and walk downhill to the bridge over the River Torridge. A short way downstream from here, on the left of the river, is Braundshill Wood where Tarka's family spent the night after being disturbed by the hunt. Carry on along the road and turn left onto the lane to Brightly Barton and then right into the field as waymarked. Walk along the edge of two fields, the second of which has been fenced off, and follow the footpath, straight on, which joins an old green lane. Follow this to the road and continue straight across Woolridge Cross (turn left here to visit the Devon Wildlife Trust reserve at Halsdon Wood) and on to Dolton village.

MAP 7

Turn right as you enter Dolton and follow the road round in front of the church, leave the village and take the footpath on the left through the iron gate, passing through fields to Ham Farm and continue to Staple Cross. At Staple Cross take the surfaced track to Staple Farm and skirt around to the right of the cattle pens then bear right through the field. Walk over the footbridge, cross the field going uphill and carry on to the muddy track that leads to Upcott.

Turn left onto the road as Upcott and then take the next footpath that follows the lane on the right. Leave the lane through the third gate on the left and diagonally cross the next two fields to the footbridge. Go over bridge and walk through this field, avoiding Coombe Farm and bear right along the old track. Stay on the track, which skirts the field, crossing the road at Coombe Cottage and carry on until you reach Eastpark Farm. Turn right out of the farmyard and follow the track to the village of Iddesleigh. Walk through the village and turn left opposite the church following the signpost for Week. After about $^3/_4$km ($^1/_2$ mile) turn right onto the footpath along the lane, follow this and pass through a gate carrying straight on across the field. Go through the next gate and follow the hedge towards Rectory Farm, walk through the farm and turn left onto the concrete track.

MAP 8

Keep straight on past Parsonage Gate and follow the road, passing the gateway to Nethercott House on the right. Just after the crossroads sign turn right through the gateway and follow this driveway towards Nethercott Barton. Turn right through the gate as you reach the farm buildings, cross the field following the hedge on your left and turn left along the green lane. At the bottom of the lane pass through the two gateways and fields to the wooden footbridge over the River Okement. Cross the river and turn left following the sunken lane up the hill. Go through a gate and turn right alongside the hedgerow, then left through the next gate and head uphill towards the barn roof before crossing the stile on the left next to the field gate.

Cross the field diagonally towards the oak trees on the right and then pass through the small orchard using the stiles. Turn left along the track, go through Groves Fishleigh and cross the fields using the stiles. Follow the cleared track through the trees, cross the stream and leave the woods through the gate. Carry straight on keeping the hedge on your right at first then pass through the gateway immediately ahead continuing uphill across this next field. Turn left onto the road through the gate and follow this to the main A386, cross this and follow the road opposite that takes you through Hatherleigh churchyard. Turn right out of the

MAP 6 A and B

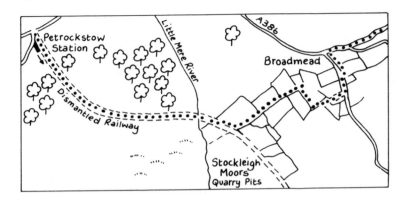

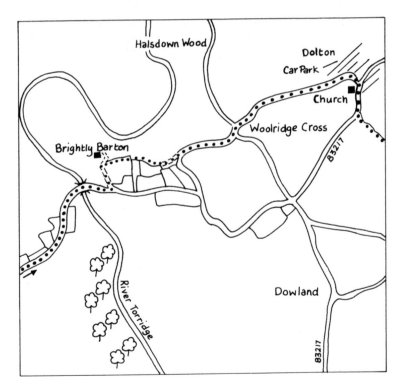

Section 4: R. Okement and Dartmoor, Petrockstowe to Dolton

MAP 7

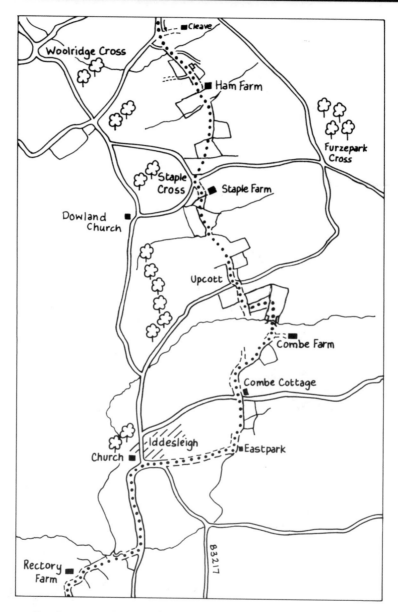

Section 4: R. Okement and Dartmoor, Ham Farm to Rectory Farm

MAP 8

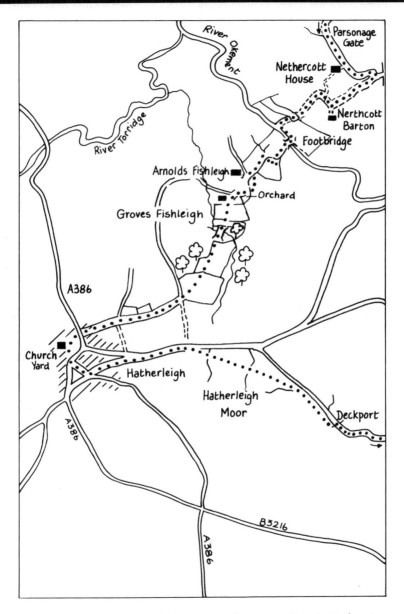

Section 4: R. Okement and Dartmoor, Parsonage Gate to Deckport

churchyard and walk into the town square. Hatherleigh has a number of shops, pubs and other places of interest to visit. Leave Hatherleigh along High Street on the opposite side of the road and downhill of the square. At the cross roads bear left along Victoria Road and walk uphill out of the town.

Take the second bridleway on the right that crosses Hatherleigh Moor, passing through two bridle gates and two field gates. On reaching the road turn right and carry on this road heading south-east.

MAP 9 + 10

Follow the road for about 3km (1.8 miles). After 1.5 miles turn right to Cadham, then continue for half a mile before turning left along the track that leads to Higher Cadham Farm. At the farmyard bear right to leave through the iron gate and cross the two fields downhill towards the river Okement. Go over the footbridge, turn right and follow the footpath upstream until you reach a road at Jacobstowe Mill. Turn right, cross the arched bridge and then follow the main road (A3072) to Jacobstowe. Follow the signs for Okehampton (A3072) and turn immediately left along the minor county road. Follow this road and after about 3km (2 miles) turn left into the Forestry Commission's Abbeyford Woods shortly after Goldburn Cross.

Follow the waymarked permissive path through the woods and turn right when you reach the road. A short way up the hill turn left along the track and follow this path to the B3217, crossing the River Okement on the way. Turn right and follow the road into Okehampton turning right at the main road to get to the town centre, with a good shopping centre and other places of interest.

From Okehampton either plan your own route across the Moor to Cranmere Pool and back to Sticklepath along the Taw Valley, or follow the route of the 'Two Museums Walk', described below, which cuts across the northern fringes of the moor (there is a Two Museums Walk leaflet available from Tourist Information Centres).

The walk to Cranmere Pool is across open moorland, where weather conditions are subject to sudden changes, even in the summer, and should not be tackled by those without the appropriate clothing and equipment, in particular map and compass.

MAP 9

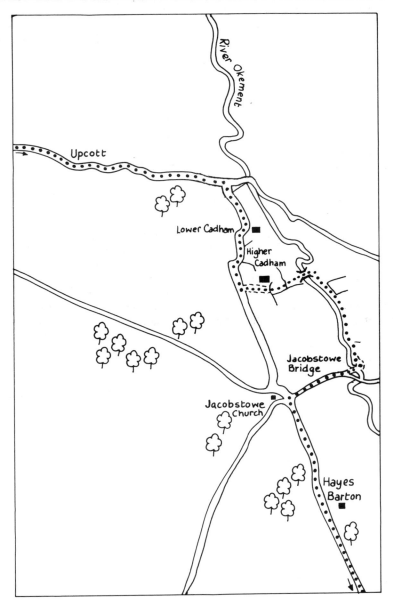

Section 4: R. Okement and Dartmoor, Upcott to Hayes Barton

MAP 10

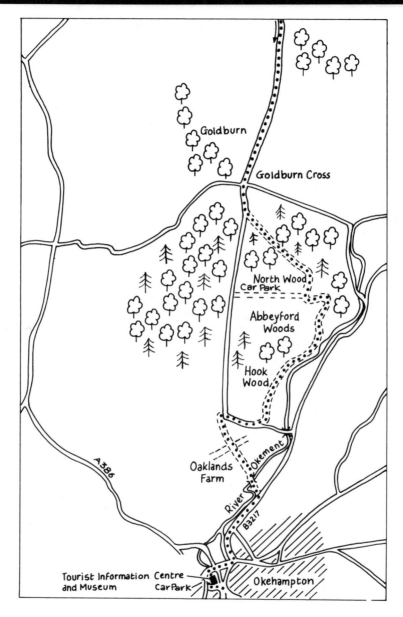

Section 4: R. Okement and Dartmoor, Goldburn to Okehampton

SECTION 5 RIVER TAW AND BARNSTAPLE

By pools and waterfalls and rillets the river Taw grew, flowing under steep hills that towered high above ... the sun rose like an immense dandelion. The grasses, the heather, the lichens, the whortleberry bushes, the mosses, the boulders, everything in front of Tarka vanished as though drowned or dissolved in a luminous strange sea, all glowing and hid in a mist of sun-fire.

The river hurried round the base of the cleave, on whose slopes stunted trees grew, amid rocks, and scree that in falling had smashed the trunks and torn out the roots of willows, thorns and hollies. It wandered away from the moor, a proper river with bridges, brooks, islands and mills.

Born of clouds the Taw hurries away north-north-east through the plateau where ling, heather and whortleberry grow. The latter, also called cloudberry, produces sweet purple berries in July and August giving local people a profitable sideline years ago 'picking hurts' or 'wurts' for pies and jam.

Belstone is as close to wilderness as any habitation in England, a true moorland village yet with the hospitality of pub, restaurant and cafe, which had already made it popular a century ago. The Taw travels down Belstone Cleave, pronounced 'claive' in the dialect, a rocky valley grown with stunted trees and bushes and ready to produce sudden slalems from thunder cloudbursts. Tarka fought here with the gang of stoats (once known as fitches or vairs in Devon), led by 'Swagdagger', a sort of animal tribe or highwaymen, in his journey downstream. Tumbling waters once provided power for the foundry, serge cloth and corn milling. At Sticklepath Foundry tools such as axes, saws, spades, scythes, and sickles are made and water still turns its old machines as a working museum.

The Taw was considered to be the principal river of this area of Devon, not so much for its length of fifty miles (compared with the seventy of the Torridge), but for its great appetite in swallowing so many other rivers and streams, principally the Yeo, Little Dart, Bullow Brook and Dalch. Records reveal a charming story about an old dog-otter known as 'Lapford Jimmy' who, for some reason, was never hunted and was said to die of old age. He was often observed playing on the weir-sill at Lapford towards dusk, sliding down and returning to the top again and again. The Taw's finest conquest comes from the Mole at Junction Pool, and it is then replete and deep, a fine river for salmon, trout and otters in days gone by. The hunted otter was often lost at Junction Pool, due to the depth of water and hidden holts. Tarka had his own adventures here where he was nearly drowned by an enormous eel which hid in a sunken bullock's skull having been half blinded by a fish-hook. Just up the road at Head Barton, back up the Mole, is the mill that was used in the Rank film of *Tarka* made in 1977, the actual Town Mill at Torrington being unsuitable. At that time it was still in its original state and the technical crew refurbished the wheel so that the otter playing Tarka could hide up in it during the final hunt, to be catapulted out among the hunt and followers when the millers returned to work after lunch. Recently the area has become a trout farm.

To otter hunters the Taw was called 'the gentleman's river' because it had become most accessible by road and rail, with frequent refreshment houses, many of which still exist, and still serve solid Devon country fare. Today the same railway line, now named The Tarka Line, operates from Exeter to Barnstaple and has stops at Eggesford three miles above Junction Pool, as well as several other places.

Farther downstream in the book, Tarka was hunted at 'Spady Gut' near Bishop's Tawton and had a near fatal encounter with his arch enemy, Deadlock, and the little terrier Bite'm who hung so fiercely onto Tarka's tail.

The Taw arrives at Barnstaple quay, its banks silty with the faint khaki colours of tidal mud. The old name, Barum, was of Roman origin. This is North Devon's capital, with low but solid buildings of sandstone and brick and a magnificent stone 'long bridge' held up by fourteen piers. Next to this is the old athenaeum, now the Museum of North Devon, which gives much background history of rural life, as well as tourist information. HW regularly frequented the old ale houses, the Barnstaple and North Devon Club, the old cinema (now a Bingo Hall), the bookshops, cafes and indoor market in his search for companionship and material on Devon life. His eightieth birthday party was held in the Imperial Hotel in the town's centre.

MAPS AND ROUTE DETAILS

SECTION 5 RIVER TAW AND BARNSTAPLE
OKEHAMPTON TO EGGESFORD

48 Kilometres (30 miles) or 34 kilometres (21 miles)

MAP 11A

Between Okehampton and Sticklepath this section passes through Dartmoor National Park. Within the Park the Trail is not waymarked since it either crosses open moorland or follows clear signposted paths on the Two Museums Walk.

Leave the Tourist Information Centre (behind the White Hart Hotel), walking along the passage next to the Museum of Dartmoor Life, then through the car park at the back and turn left along the road (Jacob's Pool). Turn right at the end of this road and follow the main road (Mill Road) past the Post Office and towards the Moor. On reaching a mill, Town Mills, climb the steps alongside, turn sharp right into Courtenay Road and follow the signs to the Ball Hill Path. At the end of the road go through the gate on the the Ball Hill footpath, following this through the fields, across the track, into the woods as far as the pumping station. When you reach the track, turn left, following the sign to Exeter Road and take the first right turn under the railway line and the new Okehampton bypass. Continue along this road for approximately 400m ($^1/_4$ mile) and take the footpath through the metal gate on your right signposted 'Road near Cleavehouse'. Cross the small granite clapper bridge and follow the footpath uphill on the left side of the hedge. Keep the field boundary to your right, through a granite gateway and over a stile, until you reach the road coming out just below a cattle grid.

Turn right on to this road and follow it into Belstone village.

Leave Belstone by the road that passes the Tors Pub leading to the common above Belstone Cleave. Bear left as you leave the buildings and take the rough track, right, down into the Cleave itself. Turn left at the bottom of the hill, cross the footbridge, turn left again and follow the hedge to your right which leads up the valley side. After a short distance, turn left off the main track, following a path on a course parallel to the river below. Fork left again after 20 metres along the course of an old leat that served the Ivy Tor Mine in the valley. After about 300 metres (330 yds) the path bears left, down towards the river and continues along the bank until you come to the site where the water wheel was located for draining Ivy Tor Mine, marked by stonework on the right of the path. Follow the path, passing Ivy Tor exposed on your right, until you reach the footbridge which you cross. It was here in Belstone Cleave that Tarka fought over a rabbit kill with Swagdagger and his

MAP 11 A and B

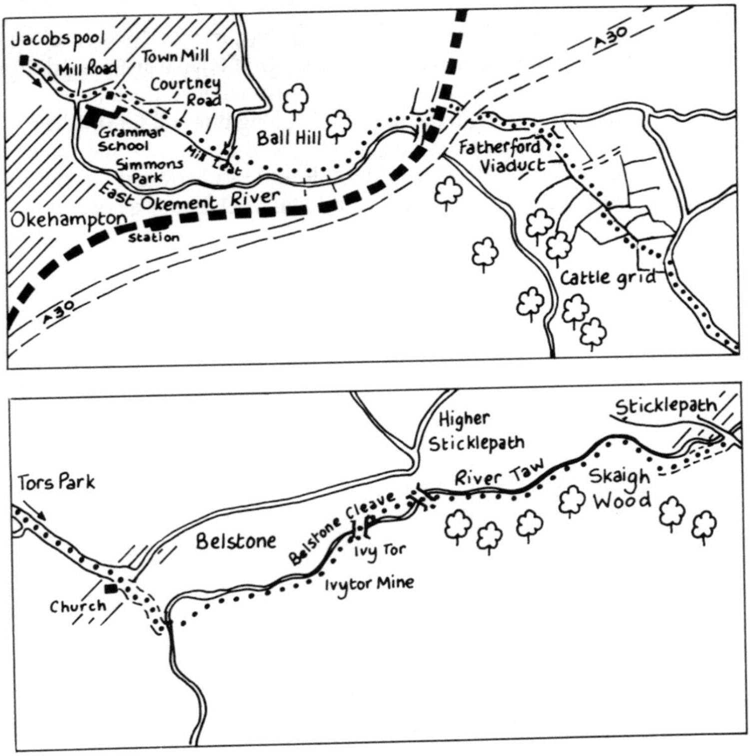

Section 5: R. Taw and Barnstaple, Okehampton to Sticklepath

fellow stoats. Continue downstream until you see a signpost; follow the direction to Sticklepath. Cross the next footbridge then continue downstream, passing a weir and Cleave Mill on the opposite bank, keep to the track as it leaves the river then follow the signpost that will take you to Sticklepath and the A30, a good stopping point for refreshments.

MAP 12

Leave Sticklepath by turning left onto the minor road at the eastern end of the bridge over the River Taw. After a very short distance take the green lane that heads uphill on your left just opposite the thatched cottage. This lane takes you to South Tawton where you rejoin the road, turning left to pass in front of the church and then following the road straight on in a northerly direction crossing the new A30 on the way to Taw Green. Here follow the road straight on and then bear left taking the road that loops round to Wyke Moor Cross where you turn left to head north again, passing the grassland research station at North Wyke.

MAP 13

Stay on this road for another 2 km (1.2 miles) before turning right along the B3215. At Newland Cross leave the road and take the footpath through the iron gate on the left just before the bridge. This path follows the River Taw downstream. On reaching the road again continue heading roughly north by following the road immediately opposite the unusual turnstile type gate you have just passed through. Stay on this road until a short way past Bridge Farm where a track bears off to the right on a sharp left hand bend in the road. Walk along this and follow the footpath over the stile on your left that takes you across a field before entering some woods on the river bank. Leave the wood over the stile and head straight on, crossing the track, still following the river northwards until you reach Bailey's Ford.

MAP 14

At Bailey's Ford go through the gate and follow the green lane that continues in a northerly direction gradually going uphill to Bondleigh Wood. Just beyond here turn right and follow the road down hill and around to the left that brings you to Bondleigh Bridge. At this T-junction turn left, cross the road and take the footpath on the right through the gate, following this straight on across the field and alongside the river bank. This path bears left away from the river just over the third stile and crosses the field to go over a footbridge, through the cottage garden back to a road. Turn right along this lane, passing the Woodland Trust Reserve and carry on for about 1½ km (1 miles) to Taw Green. At Taw Green turn right and follow this road for a short distance to the B3220; this is a busy road so care needs to be taken. Turn right and follow the main road, passing Taw Bridge Cottage on your right, cross the river and take the footpath on the left that takes you once again in a northerly direction, following the river downstream.

This path crosses the smallholding area and goes over two stiles in the corner, between the line of evergreen trees, before entering the fields. Continue roughly north-east across the pasture field towards the gate where the route turns left and follows the hedgebank towards the river. Cross the stiles into the next field and continue following the hedge banks until you reach a green lane. Turn right along this until you emerge into another field.

MAP 15

Turn left and follow the tracks across the field and through the gate. Carry straight on with the hedge on your left to come to the river bank which you now follow. On approaching Westacott Wood, leave the river bank and go over the stile to follow the track along the edge of the wood back to a road. Turn left along the road, cross the river over Coldridge Bridge and take the footpath through the squeeze stile across the field to the footbridge. After crossing this bridge and stile the path bears left and heads towards the derelict Wood Farm, pass in front of the old buildings and follow the track down through the trees to the Forestry Commission's Burrowcleave Wood. The Trail follows the forest road through the wood before bearing right along a footpath that continues following the hedgebank on your right hand side. This path take you all the way through the plantation, crossing a small stream on the way. On reaching the hunting gate at the far side of the wood, cross the field to a stile opposite and follow the path that passes through the gate in front of you, keeping the hedge on your right until you once again reach a county road. Turn left and go up the hill to Park Mill Cross.

Here, turn right and immediately left to follow the bridleway through Hawkridge Farm, turning left at the bottom of the hill to go through Wiselands Wood. On approaching Chenson Bridge turn left along the footpath that takes you parallel with the River Taw once more. After crossing two fields this path turns uphill to follow a track leading to Trenchard Farm. At Trenchard turn right along the road to Eggesford Fourways where the route turns right off the road along the track which takes you to Eggesford Barton. Here, walk around the front of the Barton and carry on along the track, passing the church and turning right at the T-junction. On the way you pass Eggesford gardens, an excellent place to stop for a cup of tea whilst waiting for your train to take you to Barnstaple. Walk down the hill on this road that takes you to Eggesford Station on the main A377.

MAP 12

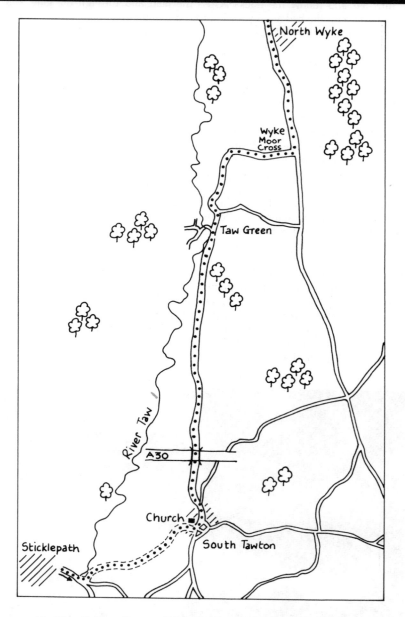

Section 5: River Taw and Barnstaple, Sticklepath to North Wyke

MAP 13

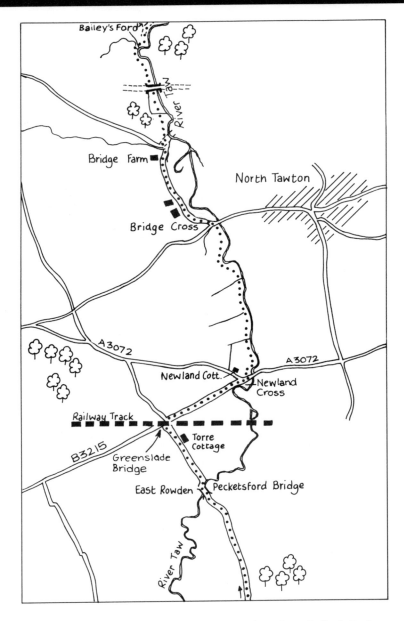

Section 5: River Taw and Barnstaple, North Wyke to Bailey's Ford

MAP 14

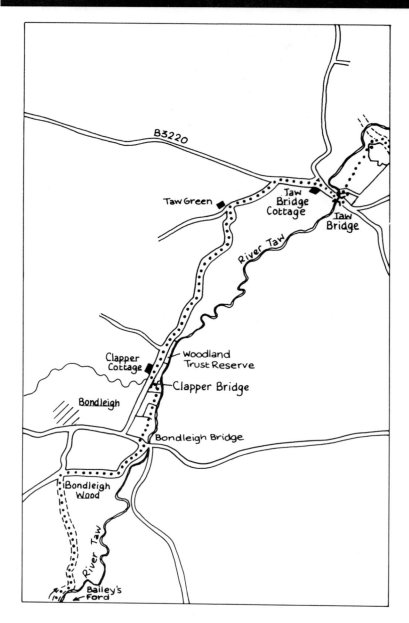

Section 5: River Taw and Barnstaple, Budleigh to Taw Bridge

MAP 15

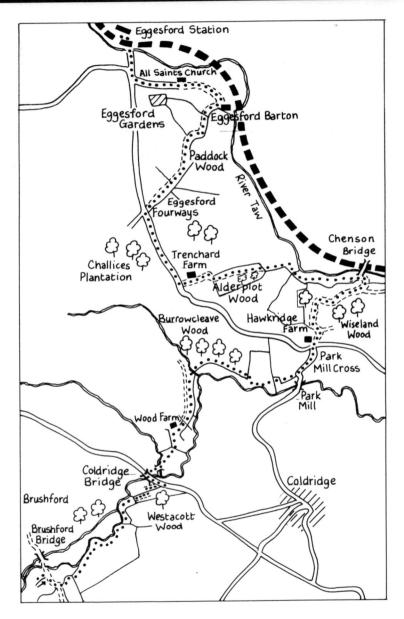

Section 5: River Taw and Barnstaple, Taw Bridge to Eggesford

Eggesford Station

Landkey

SECTION 6 EXMOOR FRINGES

Through the soft pasture ground the river roamed, coiling and uncertain. The tide-water filling it gleamed dully like a seal's hide, greyish brown and yellow freckled ... The flood tide took Tarka two miles up the river to the railway bridge. He walked up the gut that emptied a small brook from the east-lying valley beyond. Travelling up the brook, under the mazzard orchards growing on the northern slope of the valley, he reached a great hollow in the hillside, shut in with trees and luminous as the sky, for the hollow was a flooded limestone quarry.

Returning on the Taw on the opposite (eastern) bank, the Trail strikes east towards the edges of Exmoor, along Landkey Brook. Deep wooded valleys, water shaded by alder and oak trees, steep hillside meadows grazed by sheep and cattle, ribbons of flowers and butterflies in many months of the year, tied into bows around villages of white cob and thatch; all unfold before the traveller. Venn Quarry lies in austere loneliness on the northern side behind trees, a steep hollow with forty feet of water. Lime burners' cottages and a kiln with chimney once stood here. The quarry is still worked but it is all noisy lorries and bustle nowadays.

Just beyond Landkey the old railway line led from Barnstaple to Taunton and much of its former route is now the new road. At one point it uses the one-hundred-foot-high viaduct across the river Bray near East Buckland, spanning Castle Hill estate's deer park, the seat of the Fortescue family.

When steam trains crossed the viaduct, light from the firebox reflected in the Bray's pools; these were named the fireplay pools by HW. He lived for ten years at Shallowford, a tenant of Lord Fortescue, and here studied salmon, writing *Salar the Salmon* and many other Devon books. Five of his children were reared in the valley at the cottage by Humpy Bridge, one of his sons was educated at West Buckland.

Many of the old oak woods have in the past one hundred years been replaced by spruce and pine, as elsewhere in Devon. Buzzards are breeding successfully again after their demise in the 1950s to '70s. The road crosses open moorland where red deer are quite common. The Exmoor streams have carved deep ravines over thousands of years, the 'pack ponies' wore the lanes deep before tarmac sealed them and with hedge banks thrown high on either side, they can present cresta-runs on their severe gradients in hard winter conditions, especially around the village of Charles. Shale quarries are still used and blasting rocks the cottages hanging precariously over deeply gorged streams. Here the farmland is like an enormous green blancmange, the slopes sliding into woods and valleys.

The banks are rich in flowers; toadflax and tansy, betony and rosebay, names that ring like the names of the hounds in *Tarka*. Sometimes beech hedges ribbon the roads for mile after mile, often there is a mixture of shrubs like holly, hazel, hawthorn and honeysuckle. This is where that fabled slower pace of life exists. All the while the climb continues northwards to the heights of Exmoor.

SECTION 6 EXMOOR FRINGES – BARNSTAPLE TO LOWER HALL

28 kilometres (17½ miles)

MAP 16A

Turn right out of the railway station, follow the access road to the main road and turn right towards Barnstaple town centre. Cross the Long Bridge over the River Taw, pass around the front of the Museum of North Devon and turn left onto the footpath that follows the riverbank. Continue alongside the river and fork left where the path passes under the North Devon Link Road, towards Pill Lane. On reaching the main road (A377) turn right, cross the road and walk along the pavement into Bishop's Tawton. Turn left up School Lane, in front of the white school buildings and take the footpath next to the playing field. At the T-junction with the next lane (Easter Street) turn right and then left at the next T-junction into Sentry Lane. Follow this lane, go over the stile on the left and follow the footpath across the fields along the valley to Venn Quarry. The stream in the bottom of this valley is Landkey Brook which Tarka travelled up after being separated from his mate, White-tip, in a fight with ferrets in a timber yard.

MAP 16B

Take the permissive path over the stile and turn left onto the track in the field. Follow the permissive waymarks until you reach the road. Turn left, downhill, towards the quarry entrance and then right onto the footpath opposite. Follow this footpath through woods then fields and turn right onto the road, bear right, cross the bridge and continue to the house on the left. Take the footpath just beyond this, cross three fields, turn left onto the road and walk down into Landkey. For services turn left up into the village. Otherwise continue by crossing the main road into Tanner's Lane. Take the footpath on the left through the playing field, and cross the stream.

MAP 17A

Cross two stiles and turn right along the road then immediately left to go under the Link Road. Take the lane signposted 'Birch' and follow this past Stepfort and up to Birch Farm. Pass through the farmyard and follow the bridleway through the small gate and along the field boundaries to Gunn.

MAP 17B

At Gunn turn right along the road, passing in front of a row of cottages, then right again down the lane next to the chapel. At Sandick Cross, turn left along the hedged lane (signposted West Buckland). Follow this lane for a mile, pass Taddiport Farm, and turn left at the T-junction to West Buckland. At West Buckland fork left, cross the road and take the footpath on the right alongside the building and across the field.

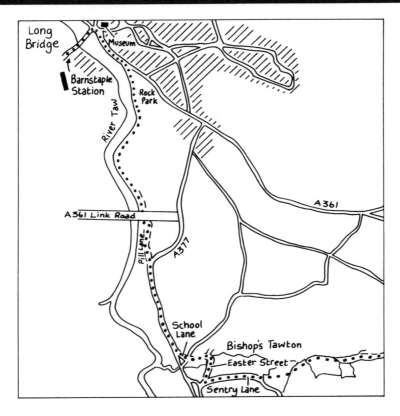

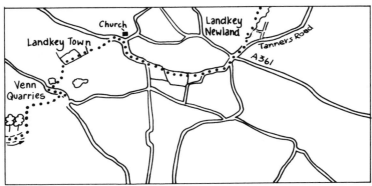

Section 6: Exmoor fringes, Barnstaple to Landkey

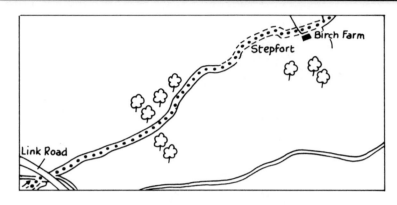

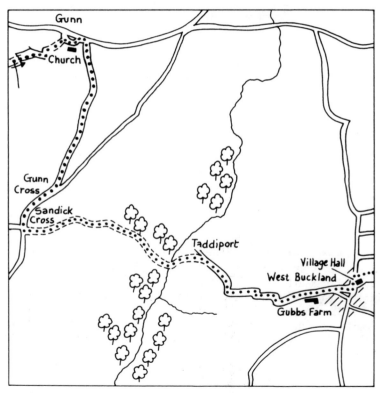

Section 6: Exmoor fringes, Landkey to West Buckland

MAP 18

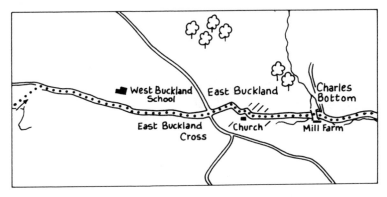

Section 6: Exmoor fringes, West Buckland to Charles Bottom

MAP 18

Go over the next stile and cross the field diagonally to the gate onto the road and turn right. Continue along the road, passing West Buckland School, to East Buckland Cross. Go straight over the crossroads and follow the road through the village.

Leave the village, pass through Mill Farm, cross the bridge over the stream and fork right to Blakewell Farm.

MAP 19

Pass through the gate across the lane and turn right at the T-junction then left along the footpath that takes you down into the valley and alongside the River Bray. Stay on this until you reach the end of the wood, pass through two gates with a small stream between them, and then turn uphill across the field to Grasspark. Go through the gate and turn right through the farm to the road. Turn right onto the road and down the steep hill to the B3226. Cross the road and continue over Newtown Bridge to Rock's Head Cross.

Turn left here through the black, wooden gate and go along the track into Barton Wood. Follow the permissive forest tracks and cross the Little Owl River by the footbridge and continue north along the track to the gate out of the wood. Turn left onto the road, pass Withygate and take the footpath on the left across the footbridge and up the hill to Lower Hall Farm. Pass through the farm and turn right onto the road. This road marks the boundary of Exmoor National Park which you will now be walking through until leaving it at Combe Martin. Within the Park the Trail is waymarked with white otter paw prints incorporated into the National Park's footpath signs. From here, there are no main settlements until you reach Lynmouth, 15 miles away, so be prepared.

MAP 19

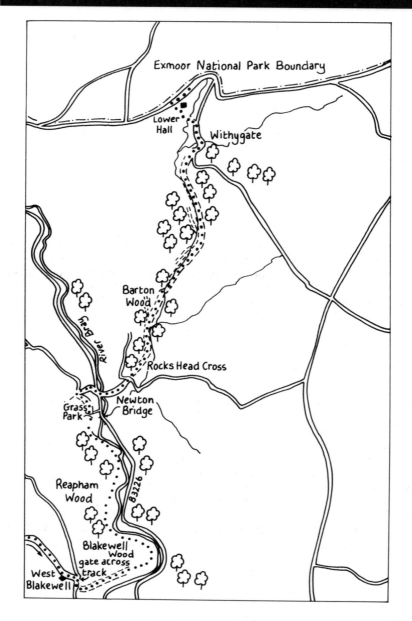

Section 6: Exmoor fringes, Charles Bottom to Lower Hall

SECTION 7 EXMOOR

When the bee's feet shake the bells of the heather and the ruddy strings of the sap-stealing dodder are twined about the green spikes of the furze, it is summertime on the commons.

Exmoor is the high country of the winds, which are to the falcons and the hawks: clothed by whortleberry bushes and lichens and ferns and mossed trees in the goyals, which are to the foxes, the badgers, and the red deer: served by rain-clouds and drained by rock clittored streams, which are to the otters. . . . Within the moor is the Forest, a region high and treeless, where sedge grasses grown on the slopes to the sky.

A tarn lies under two hills, draining water from a tussock-linked tract of bog called The Chains. The tarn is deep and brown and still, reflecting rushes and reeds at its sides, the sedges of the hills, and the sky over them.

Exmoor is a glorious wilderness, even in the 1990s. Over three thousand years ago Celtic man left his chieftains entombed in tumuli on the heights called Chains, where clouds drag their ropes of rain from the ocean to recharge the sponge of peat that is Exmoor. Like elvers, the rivers wriggle away; the Exe eastwards, Mile and Bray southwards, West Lyn, Hoar Oak and Farley Waters northwards. For HW this was his spiritual home. Via the Devonshire Shapcotes, some of whom had long ago been shepherds on this high moorland plateau, he claimed blood descent and therefore an inherited love and knowledge of the moors.

From the existence of ancient man in this wilderness he found the reassurance of an even deeper link to primordial roots and he coined the phrase 'Ancient Sunlight': a far away but brilliant race-memory that had given him his insight into the life of man, otter, bird and fish. Just as the peat had given rise to stored energy from sunlight thousands of years before, so too were handed on the seeds of divine creation from ancestors.

Throughout his life he loved to walk up here, though he was always a little fearful of straying off the path and falling into a bog, no doubt remembering the fate of Carver Doone. For it was up here that the seventeenth-century brigand, the anti-hero of R.D. Blackmore's novel *Lorna Doone*, sank to his doom in the quaking bogs.

Many times HW stated that he wanted to die on the Chains, where he would walk until exhausted and then lie down and die like one of the red deer stags, or he imagined a great Wagnerian scene where he would build a huge bonfire and throw himself into the flames. This he turned into the climax of *The Gale of the World*, the last novel of his long fifteen volume sequence *A Chronicle of Ancient Sunlight*, where he graphically describes the great storm that led to the disastrous flooding of Lynmouth, when nine inches of rain fell on the Chains in a very few hours.

In the early 1800s a Mr Knight from Worcestershire purchased 10,262 acres of the land for £50 000 and built the roads more or less as we know them today. Before that the moor was crossed with packhorse trackways running haphazardly through the difficult terrain. Knight tried to mine iron-ore, using Welsh and Cornish miners, but lost much of his money. Gangs of Irishmen built an embankment called 'Paddy's Fence' just below the Chains and he started work on a canal to assist in the transport of iron-ore.

Pinkworthy (pronounced Pinkery) Pond, another of Knight's schemes, once covered seven acres but is considerably less today. There is a story that he built it for his son so that a model yacht could be sailed, but more likely it was to provide water to feed the canal and to provide power for a mill. Tarka watched a raven catching frogs in the pond. Otters visit the pond as they did in Tarka's day, and ravens are to be seen, as well as buzzards and kestrels. In *On Foot in Devon* published in 1933, where HW described a walk he had undertaken round the entire Devon coast, he states that he once saw fourteen ravens flying together up here, also merlins, and that black game lived on the moor with their female grey hens.

Curlew may still occasionally breed, although dogs brought here by walkers and allowed to run loose, are likely to limit their success more and more. The liquid bubbling song of the curlew, uttered during a star or moonlit night of early summer, is one of the most beautiful experiences of the moor. Meadow pipits and skylarks breed, while in the valley woodlands goldcrests and ring ouzels may be seen.

The Moor, a National Park, is a place dominated by bell heather with cotton grass, and patches of soft rush. Efforts to plough and lime the habitat were still being carried out in the 1970s but it is now largely regarded as a place where human intrusion should be kept to a minimum. Red deer wander the edges of the moor, harbouring in the steep wooded valleys. Foxes and badgers, stoats, weasels and field voles, all have their hunting grounds over this remnant of ancient England.

The way northwards off the moor is by way of the remarkable Hoar Oak Tree. Apparently the original Hoar Oak (which can be dated pre-1300) fell down through decay in 1658, and was replaced directly. This tree fell down in 1916, and was again replaced. HW writing in the mid-1920s says Tarka passes 'the Hoar Oak, whose splintered stump, black as a shadow with the moon behind, glistered with the track of slugs. Near the Hoar Oak stood a sapling, caged from the teeth and horns of deer, a little tree by the grave of its father'. Its importance was a boundary marker for the former Royal Forest in a region where natural boundary marks are rare. In earlier times it was one of only two trees in the 'Forest', for the original meaning of forest was not of a place of trees but of a place outside, i.e. a wild place.

The way leads on past ancient hut circles, tumuli and enclosures, and downwards between leaping rivers to the sea. Tarka and his arch enemy, the dreaded hound Deadlock, fought a battle in these rivers, a minor crescendo, a foretelling of what is to come, as they are swept together over a foaming torrent in a Holmes/Moriarty confrontation which the two protagonists only just survived.

MAP 20

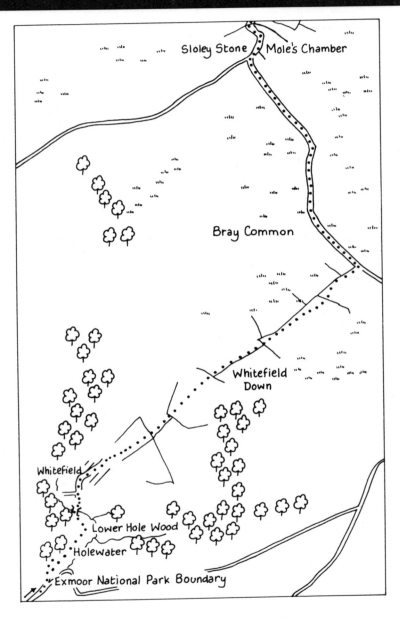

Section 7: Exmoor, Holewater to Mole's Chamber

SECTION 7 EXMOOR – LOWER HALL TO LYNMOUTH

24 kilometres (15 miles)

MAP 20

A short way along the road, take the footpath up the track on the left and follow this through the woods, leaving through the hunt gate. Cross the footbridge over the river and go up the hill to the road. Turn right out of the gate and follow the road through Whitefield Farm, bear left and take the footpath on the right that crosses Whitefield Down in a north-easterly direction. On reaching the road, turn left and continue to Mole's Chamber, turn right off the road on the bend and pass through the iron gate.

MAP 21

Follow the bridleway with the wire sheep fence on either side, bearing left until you come to a wooden gate, go through this and cross the field to the next gate keeping the stream on your right-hand side. Go through this gate and continue following the bridlepath north to the B3358. Cross the road and take the bridleway to Wood Barrow. On reaching Wood Barrow Gate, turn right and follow the path eastwards to Pinkworthy Pond. Tarka spent time here before being disturbed by the Stag Hunt and crossing the Chains to travel down the Hoar Oak Water.

Leave Pinkworthy in an easterly direction following the hedge bank and signs towards Exe Head.

MAP 22

Here, the source of the River Exe, turn left through the gate and follow an old bank till the path bears left into the Hoar Oak Water valley. Carry on, crossing the stream at the foot of Long Chains Combe and follow it downstream till you are opposite the Hoar Oak Tree, a stunted oak tree growing within a small fenced enclosure on the valley side opposite. Ford the stream again, pass through the gate in the fence to the left of the tree and carry on following the stream until you come to a field boundary running uphill to your right, at right angles to the river.

MAP 23

Follow this boundary up the hill, turn left at the corner and follow the line of the rough track, keeping the field boundaries on your left-hand side. Carry on following this line until the hedge banks form a funnel that leads you off the moor, through a field gate and onto a track.

From here to Lynmouth, the Trail follows the Two Moors Way, waymarked with a black and white symbol incorporating the letters M and W.

48

MAP 21

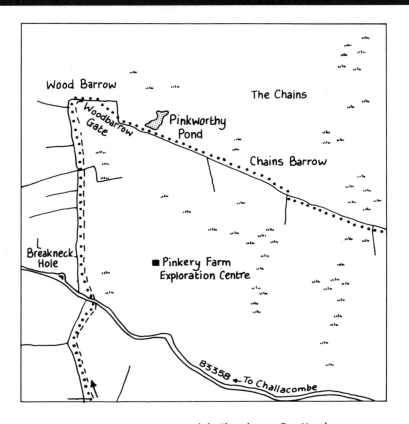

Section 7: Exmoor, Mole's Chamber to Exe Head

When the track brings you to the metalled road turn left, then bear right at the fork in the road to head for Scoresdown. Cross the Hoar Oak over Smallcombe Bridge and turn right onto the permissive track through National Trust land to Hillsford Bridge. At Hillsford Bridge turn left and take the A39, signposted 'Lynton and Barnstaple', for a short distance before turning right through the gate on to the green lane signposted 'Footpath to Lynmouth'. Follow this path, ignoring the branches off to Watersmeet and carry on until you start to drop down into Lynmouth. The last part of this path is between some cottages and you then emerge on to the main road. Turn left along this and walk down into the town alongside the East Lyn River. Lynmouth is a popular small tourist town, with a variety of shops, cafes and accommodation.

MAP 22

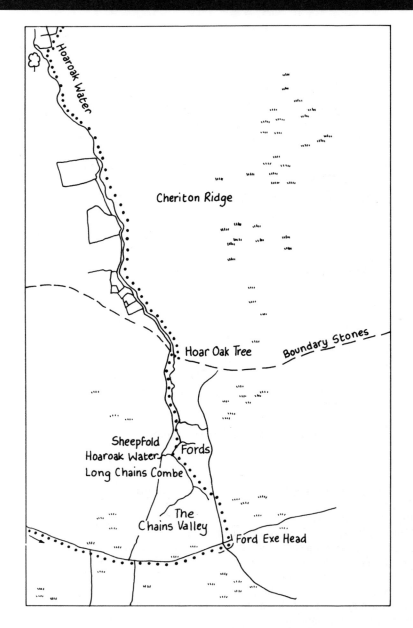

Section 7: Exmoor, Exe Head to Hoaroak Water

MAP 23

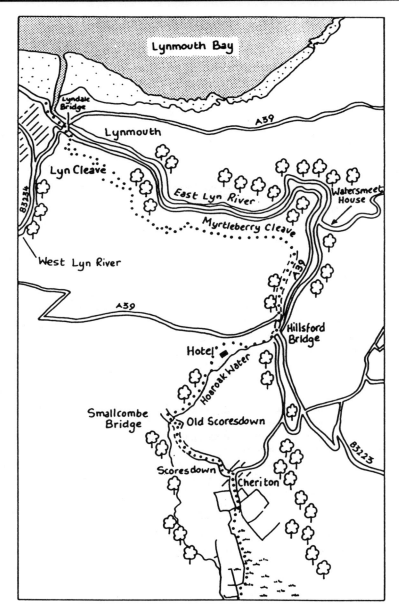

Section 7: Exmoor, Hoaroak to Lynmouth

SECTION 8 NORTH DEVON COAST

Here sunlight was shut out by the oaks and the roar of the first fall and beating back from the leaves. The current ran faster narrowing into a race with twirls and hollows marking the sunken rocks. The roar grew louder in a drifting spray. Tarka went over in the heavy white folds of the torrent. He yielded himself to the water and let it take him away down the gorge . . . reached the sea . . . vanished in a wave.

Swimming towards the sunset, Tarka went westwards, under the towering cliffs and waterfalls in whose ferny sides he liked to rest by day. A cargo steamer was passing up the Severn Sea leaving a long smudge of smoke on the horizon, where a low line of clouds billowed over the coast of Wales. Autumn's little Summer, when day and night are equal and only the woodlark sang his wistful falling song over the bracken, was ruined by the gales that tore wave and leaf and broke the sea into roar and spray and hung white ropes over the rocks. Fog hid clifftop and stars and Tarka travelled on (until) tired and buffeted by the long Atlantic rollers, he turned back under the Morte Stone, and swam to land.

Perhaps one of the reasons for *Tarka's* success as a story is the remarkable beauty and variety of the landscape through which he travels, so brilliantly interpreted by the pen. The North Devon coastline, southern shore of the Severn Sea, changes in aspect, colour and elevation almost every step of the way. Headland, cove, cliff, coombe, torrent, wave, plant and tree are constantly a marvel of fresh design.

Tarka travelled west, as we shall do; but first we visit the Victorian tourist attraction of Lynton and Lynmouth. For the lucky Edwardian tourist a narrow gauge railway was built in 1898 from Barnstaple, winding through the hills and pulled by American-built locomotives. The line was declared bankrupt in 1935 but today fragments of coach and line are painstakingly being restored.

However, the water-powered cliff railway still slides safely and majestically up and down the steep cliff which separates the two towns, a triumph of environment-friendly design. The trail takes you up the zig-zag path through the tall cliffside trees where you can stand on a bridge across the cliff railway and watch it working. Though Lynmouth has been rebuilt, the terrible floods of 1952, when nine inches of rain over Exmoor bore down this narrow gorge removing everything in its path, will never be forgotten.

The path now takes you along the clifftops, whilst Tarka, of course, swam along the shoreline. The cliffs are breeding haunts of herring gulls, black backed gulls and fulmars. Here too are peregrine falcons, which declined in numbers after the war due to pesticides and persecution but are now returning in greater numbers. A few guillemots and razorbills return to nest in hidden crevices but the puffins have gone and only a few may be found on Lundy Island which can be seen, or not seen, according to the weather, in the mid-distance. The moorland flora of gorse and heather tumbles down steep cliffs and changes to a culture of ferns and lichens growing in the cool damp flow of sea air, hanging in trailing tongues and beards on wind-blasted trees in the goyals. There are thirty six species of butterflies breeding along this north coastal zone, the rare species being six of the fritillaries – marsh, silver-washed, high brown, small pearl-bordered and pearl-bordered – as well as purple hairstreak and grayling, whilst various species of blue butterfly can be seen each in their own particular breeding season.

Climbing steeply out of Lynmouth you soon come to the wild Byronic landscape of The Valley of Rocks; then dive into the hidden shelter of Lee Bay; up to the crest; down again into the bigger Woody (or Woods as it used to be called) Bay. The path is as rolling as the high seas of the Atlantic itself.

Tarka swam as far as the mouth of the River Heddon where he slept in a disused lime-kiln for a week, exhausted after his recent battle with the hounds and with the sea. These lime-kilns are scattered along the coast. They were built in the eighteenth century in an effort to try and sweeten the acid soil of the moor for agriculture, by calcining limestone brought over from Wales by boat. Further on Tarka witnessed the dreadful occurrence when a red deer stag hunted by three staghounds all came hurtling over the cliff to smash on the rocks below.

And so onwards, past Combe Martin (HW states that the natives called it 'Koo Mart'n'), then down from the wilderness into the metropolis of Ilfracombe. HW lived here in a cul-de-sac under the shadow of the high Capstone lookout promontory from the mid-1950s to 1976 (when he was taken ill), at 4 Capstone Place where there is a plaque on the wall. The sight of his old green MG Magnette (for which he was forever getting parking fines as he was too impatient to find official spaces), and his upright white-haired figure, was familiar to all local residents. At the end of the road The Britannia Arms, hard by the quay with its fishing boats and lifeboat launching post, gave him company whenever he needed it.

The National Trust own and care for long stretches of this coastline, as they do in many other parts of Britain. Particularly beautiful is the headland of Morte Point, where thrift, sea campion, bell heather, lesser gorse, sap-sucking dodder, and the myriads of other plants that make up the green sward grow wild, but is so neatly controlled by sheep grazing that it resembles a finely kept but wild grand-scale rock garden.

Halfway along Woolacombe Sands is a cliff path up across Pickwell Down, much used by HW and his family, for it brings you to Ox's Cross, the field one mile north of the village of Georgeham which HW bought with the £100 he gained from the Hawthornden Prize awarded to *Tarka the Otter* and where he built himself first a small writing hut and later a larger studio. These buildings are maintained by his family, with the help of The Henry Williamson Society (set up in 1980 to further his literary heritage), and there are occasional small exhibitions held there. It is hoped that eventually they can be opened on a more permanent basis as a small museum. HW lived here for fifty years, writing a further 45 books after *Tarka*, and hundreds of articles. In the village of Georgeham it is possible to see Skirr Cottage where HW lived when he first moved to Devon in 1921 and where his early tales of village life were written, and Vale House where most of *Tarka* was written, and also, within yards of Skirr, his simple grave in the churchyard – simple at his own request. He had bought the plot many many years before when it became obvious that the churchyard was almost full and that future burials would take place in the cemetery half way up the hill to Ox's Cross. HW knew where he wished to rest.

Baggy Point headland, starting at Putsborough Beach at the southern end of Woolacombe Sands, was his favourite cliff walk and it was here that many of the early animal stories were based, particularly those on peregrine falcon and raven. At Baggy Point earlier in the story, Tarka and his mate Greymuzzle were frightened by the playfulness of Jarrk, the Atlantic seal, and watched a man climb down whilst his spaniel stops in fright on the path. The man (HW) enters a cave and calms the frightened seal and her cub by playing, Pied Piper fashion, 'several soft notes' on a wooden whistle, made from an elderberry stick. Perhaps HW did go down there as a young man – he certainly didn't in later years, showing extreme nervousness to the point of paranoia should anyone else decide to do so. It *is* dangerous, so do treat it with respect.

MAPS AND ROUTE DESCRIPTION

SECTION 8 NORTH DEVON COAST
LYNMOUTH TO BRAUNTON BURROWS
51 kilometres (32 miles)
MAP 24 A, B & C

Much of the coast path crosses land owned by the National Trust – please respect their byelaws when crossing their property. The Tarka Trail, now heading west, joins the coast path, waymarked with the National Trail acorn logo, leaving Lymouth next to the Information Centre on the sea front. The path zig-zags up the hill and joins North Walk. Follow this metalled road and path past several hotels and around Hollerday Hill to the Valley of Rocks. As you round a corner and see Castle Rock in front of you, turn to pass to the landward side of this buttress and join the road. Follow the road for about 2½ km (1½m), passing Lee Abbey and past a left turn signposted Slatenslade then, after a further 180m (200 yds), turn right into the woods. Continue along this track, crossing the small footbridge over the stream, until you reach a surfaced lane. Carry on along this to a sharp hairpin bend and go over the stile on the right-hand side of the lane. Keep following the path, past a small waterfall at Hollow Brook, until you are looking down into the valley at Heddon's Mouth. Below you on the other side of the river is the small, round lime kiln that Tarka used for lying up in during his journey around the coast. The path turns inland and heads down towards the valley floor where you follow the sign 'Hunter's Inn ½ mile' until reaching a footbridge on your right. Cross this, turn right, going downstream for a short distance, pass through a gate and then turn left to continue upstream. Go through another gate and look out for a path on the right that cuts away uphill, back towards the coast. Follow this path, traversing the slopes, across a dry valley and then head out on the spectacular path towards the

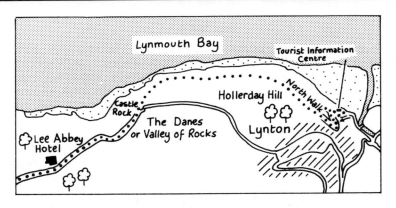

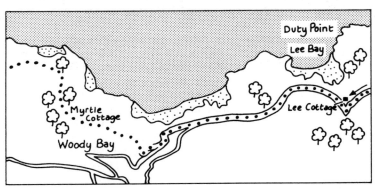

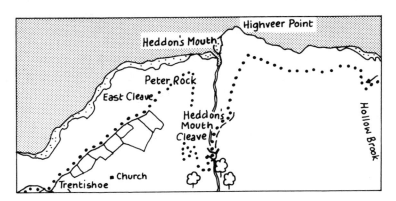

Section 8: North Devon Coast, Lynmouth to Trentishoe

55

sea and Peter Rock. The path now follows the coast again taking you to East Cleave, then turns south to reach the top of the coastal slope and follows the hedgebank at the top.

MAP 25 A, B & C

Immediately before the gully above Neck Wood, turn into the fields and follow the contours around the back of the coastal hollows. On reaching the western end there is a stile and hunt gate that lead onto a stony track. Follow this, gradually going uphill to the hedgebank, pass through the gap in the boundary and continue until joining a wide, turfed track. Follow this track as it gradually descends, through the sheep pasture to a hedgebank running across the line of the path. Turn left, following this boundary for about 100m (90 yds), pass through it, carrying on alongside the hedge for a further 180m (200 yds) and then veer right, downhill, at 45 degrees to descend into Sherrycombe. Cross over a stile and continue down the steep slope to the stream, ford this and walk up the opposite valley side. Carry on following the path to a field boundary corner and turn left to keep parallel to the cliffs. At the end of the hedgebank bear right to follow the track going north-west towards the cairn which marks the top of Great Hangman, the highest point on the South West Coast Path at 318m (1043 feet). From here head straight towards the pyramidal shape of Little Hangman, following a ridge until reaching a fence which you follow on the seaward side. Pass through a kissing gate then down some steps, over a stile and walk around the inland side of Little Hangman. Keep to the top of the coastal slopes on the seaward side of the fence, passing Wild Pear Beach below and carry on just inside a hedge. This clifftop path rises up and passes a rain shelter then a triangle of lawns leading down towards the beach.

Follow the path down until you come into the car park with the National Park Information Centre at the entrance. This is Combe Martin, a long village extending for 2 miles from the beach up the A399. Cross the car park and follow the road (A399) around the sea front, then head uphill and round the corner above the beach. Off this bend turn right along a metalled lane heading seawards. Follow this lane, turning sharp right out of the valley and along a sunken lane that brings you back to the main A399 road which you now follow on the footpath that runs parallel with it. After a short distance this path returns to the road by some wooden steps. You now follow the coastal road for about 275m (300 yds) before turning right along a small lane at the Sandycove Hotel. This lane becomes a track that you follow until reaching a stile on your right, opposite a drive on the left-hand side of the track.

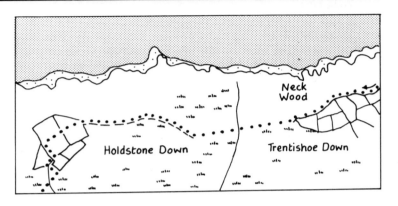

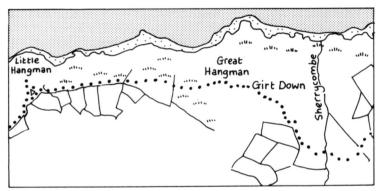

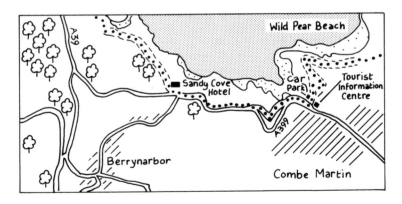

Section 8: North Devon Coast, Neck Wood to Sandy Cove

Go over this stile and walk around the next two fields on the seaward side and rejoin the main road again near Watermouth Castle. If tidal conditions allow it is possible to walk around the edge of Watermouth Bay, leaving the shore by the concrete steps on the left, but at high tide you must continue along the main road for a short distance and then cross the stile into the sycamore woods on your right. Continue, leave the woods and keep to the coastal side of the meadow then walk around Widmouth Head. From here the path takes you along the back of Samson's Bay before turning right along the cliff top to Rillage Point.

At Rillage Point the route rejoins the coastal road, at times on a separate path and partly on the verge, until reaching a picnic area. Carry on along the pavement into Hele, turning right at Hele Bay Hotel down towards the beach and then up the steps next to the toilets. The route over Hillsborough can be confusing due to frequent cliff falls and care needs to be taken to follow the coast path waymarks. On reaching the iron railings near the top of Hillsborough the path turns inland for about 100m (90 yds) and then right as you come into view of Ilfracombe again. Cross the open public spaces towards the town, walk along the edge of the harbour, bearing left at the slip and then turn right into Broad Street. At the T-junction, turn left into Capstone Road next to the Sandpiper Inn, carry on passing Henry Williamson's cottage. Turn right after about 150m (170 yds) to walk around Capstone Point.

Continue following the coast around Wilders Mouth Beach then following the signs, walk along the promenade and across the front of the park area. For services, Ilfracombe main street is left up one of the roads at right angles to the beach. Turn left, inland along the road then immediately right to climb steeply behind some ornamental gardens above the museum. This brings you to Granville Road where you go through the gate, turn right and walk along this cliff road for about 200m (220 yds) before bearing right onto an unmetalled road that takes you to Torr Walks. At the end of the track turn right, onto a concrete driveway going uphill and then bear round to the left across the grassy area to rejoin the coast path proper once more, by the National Trust sign. Turn right towards the sea along the tarmac path, continuing for some 200m (220 yds) along the cliff edge, before climbing the zig-zag path up the Seven Hills turning right at the junction on the way up. On reaching the Seven Hills, walk a short distance inland to join the wide grassy track and carry on until you see a fence ahead. Turn left, inland, to a stile and then back to the right again to continue westwards, following the farm track that was formerly the coast road from Ilfracombe to Lee. Follow this track until it becomes a lane that takes you down into Lee.

Turn right onto the road through Lee, along the back of the beach and up the hill till you see a National Trust sign for Damage Hue.

MAP 27

Here, turn right through the wicket gate and walk along the cliff top following the clearly defined path to Bull Point. On seeing the lighthouse at Bull Point head towards the left side of the enclosure, cross the road and continue in a south-westerly direction. Walk across the open grassy area then zig-zag up the small cliffs and carry on, passing between the small hills then drop down towards Rockham

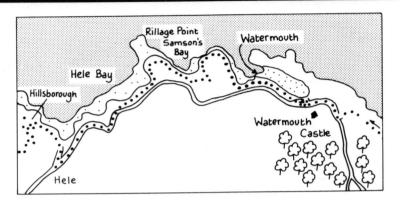

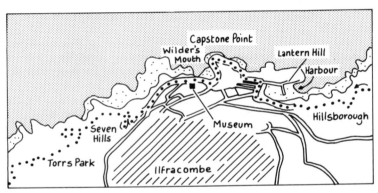

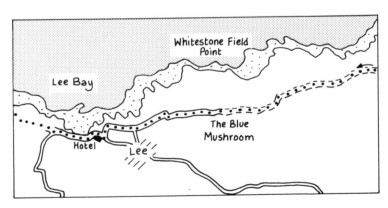

Section 8: North Devon Coast, Watermouth to Lee Bay

MAP 27

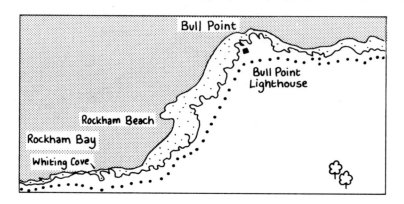

Section 8: North Devon Coast, Lee to Whiting Cove

Beach. Keep following the coast path past Whiting Cove, climbing briefly to a seat and then going downhill again to follow the path along the lower cliff slopes to Morte Point.

MAP 28

Walk around Morte Point and follow the path along the coast towards Woolacombe. When the path reaches the road, head downhill, turn right opposite the bus stop and follow the path along the front below the road. Woolacombe has a variety of services of which walkers may want to take advantage. Next to the water works, walk across the grassed area to pick up a path next to the concrete wall. Carry on through the car park to the road and turn right to walk along the road at the back of the beach past the beach shops. Fork right off the pavement when you come to a National Trust sign for Woolacombe Warren onto the bridleway that takes you behind Woolacombe Sands. Stay on this track until you fork left and go up some steps that bring you to a well-defined track. Follow this track to the inland side of Vention and keep straight on to the county road following this for about 180m (200 yds).

MAP 29

At a gateway with a stile beside it turn right and follow the track beside the field boundary to the top of the steeper slope before branching off to the right to come to the gorse covered slopes. Walk along this path at the top of the slopes out onto Baggy Point. Stay on the path to the extreme south-west corner of Baggy Point, go over a stile and follow the stony path that heads down the cliff towards the point before turning sharply back towards Croyde Bay.

Continue along the level path across the coastal slope which leads you eventually into the village street. Carry on along the lane passing the National Trust car park until you see a caravan site, turn right, walk onto the beach and head for the far southern corner. Keep to the back of the beach, crossing over a bridge half way and walk along a line of rocks just under the cliff. Stay under the cliffs across a small sandy beach and then follow the path that climbs to the cliff top. Turn right to walk along the low grass topped cliffs until Saunton Sands come into view. Walk towards the old coastguard lookout, climb up to the road, cross over and rejoin the path by walking a short distance along the road to your left. There are some concrete steps to take you up from the road to the path where you turn right and continue above and parallel to the road.

On reaching the Saunton Sands Hotel descend to the road, cross over, follow the signs to loop around the landward side of the hotel and go down the wooden steps to the seashore. The path now follows a track off the beach, through the car park and past the southern side of the houses.

Morte Point

MAP 28

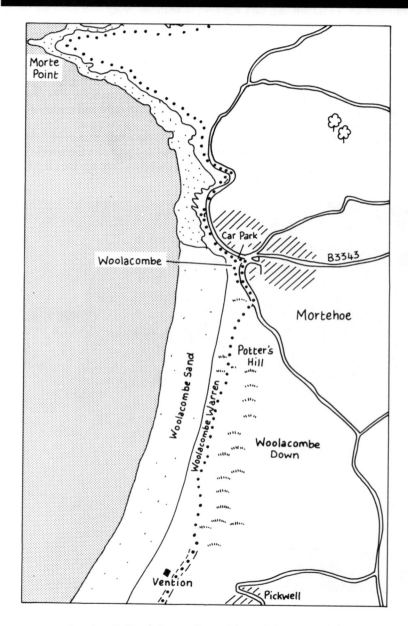

Section 8: North Devon Coast, Morte Point to Vention

MAP 29

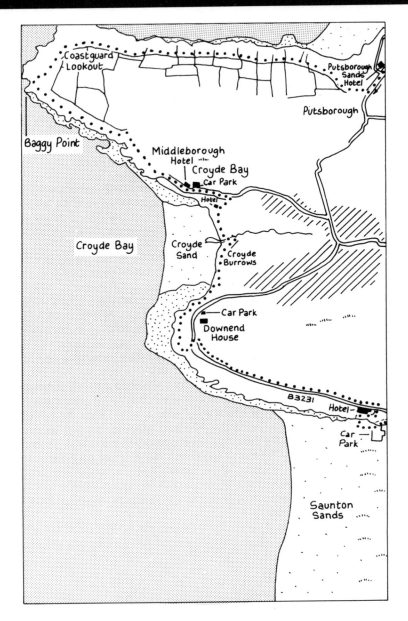

Section 8: North Devon Coast, Putsborough to Saunton

SECTION 9 BRAUNTON BURROWS AND THE ESTUARY

All day the wind shook the rusty reed-daggers at the sky, and the mace-heads were never still. The purple-ruddy beams of sunset stained the grass and the thistles of the meadow, and the tiles of the cattle-shippen under the sea-wall were the line of the sky. Westward the marshman's cottage, the linhays, the trees, the hedges, the low ragged line of the Burrows, were vanishing in a mist of fire.

The tide was ebbing, the mud slopes grey, with ruddy tricklings. In the salt turf below the sea-wall great creeks wandered with the fire of the sky.

Stand at the top of Saunton Down and look at the magnificent view of the sea, sand and dunes that make up the Braunton Burrows complex. Whether in the full golden sunlight, or at lurid sunset as described above, or in the etched silver of full moonlight, or in the smudged mistiness of bitter cold as in the 'Great Winter' scene, it is incomparable. Your spirit will be fed for leaner days of starvation.

For thousands of years the ocean washed up sea shells into the estuary of the two rivers. The waves broke them into tiny bits, the wind blew them into dunes. Eight square kilometres of shell sand, piled into hills and hummocks, makes this one of the biggest deposits of calcareous sand in the country. A seedbed so perfect for particular flowering plants that over four hundred species have been recorded on the Burrows. Some, like the marsh orchids, grow in profusion in the 'slacks' or damp dune valleys. Others, like the nationally rare (Red Data) sea stock, (*Matthiola sinuata*) grow on dry slopes, and some such as sea rocket, grow only on the very edge of the high-tide mark.

Sometimes the dunes are a vivid yellow carpet of birdsfoot trefoil, sometimes it changes to the pink of centaury, or the blue of viper's bugloss at other times to the yellow of evening primrose, or the lilac of wild thyme. Often the colours of butterflies add to this mosaic, with common blue, grayling, grizzled skipper and silver-studded blue among the thirty-four species recorded in this area. Dragonflies breed in the small pools of the marsh and ponds inland, a rare snail breeds in the dunes, and oystercatchers, curlews, ringed plovers and turnstones feed along the shore. At low tide cormorants roost in the sand at Airy Point, and the 'clockwork toys' – sanderlings – are often to be seen in winter running at the edge of the high tide like bits of blown spume.

The 'Great Winter' scene, set in the Burrows, provides what is possibly the finest writing HW ever achieved, and I make no excuse for quoting you yet another passage from Tarka.

A cold mist lay on the plains and in the hollows riming the marram grasses and the withered stems of thistles and mullein. Everything was white. The sedges and reeds of the duckponds were white, so was the rigging of the ketches in the pill. For two days and two nights the frosty vapour lay over the Burrows and then came a north wind which poured like liquid glass from Exmoor. The Icicle Spirit was coming and no terrestrial power could exorcise it. A fine powdery snow whirled out of the sky at night and the next day thicker snowflakes fell. Beyond the shaped and ever-shifting heaps of snow-sand, beyond the ragged horizon of the purple-grey sea, the sun had sunk as though it were spent in space, a dwarfed star quenching in its own steam of decay. Night was like day, for neither moon nor sun nor star was seen. The blizzard passed, and the snow lay in its pallor under the sky.

It was here that Tarka and Greymuzzle starved, their cub killed by the frost. Opposite Appledore village they caught a wild swan, only to have it stolen by Bloody Bill Brock the Badger. It was at this same place, Crow Point, that Willie Maddison, the hero of HW's tetralogy *The Flax of Dream*, in its last volume *The Pathway*, was drowned when the fishing boat he was waiting for did not materialise, and, cut off by the tide, he attempted to swim to Appledore, a death akin to that of the poet Shelley.

Before 1952 and the onset of myxomatosis, the dunes were a giant rabbit warren, and tens of thousands were caught an iron gin-traps and sent to London for the felt hat trade and the meat markets. The whole area was used as a military training ground during the war when severe erosion of the dune vegetation occurred. Tanks and infantry using machine guns and flame-throwers trained here. Amphibious vehicles landed from the estuary waters, and some unusual military hardware was tested on the local beaches. Today there are still ground manoeuvres, while nearby Chivenor Royal Air Force station flies BAC Hawks. Red flags warn of military activity and you must not enter the training area when they are flying.

In the 1920s Chivenor was a grass aerodrome and HW attempted to learn to fly here – with little success! Possibly he would not listen to the instructor, who vowed never to take him up again! I too, had my own first flying experience whilst in the school cadets, in a Tiger Moth, at Chivenor, when the view of the estuary seemed like a flow of molten lava streaming gold and smooth into the ocean.

The Burrows is a Site of Special Scientific Interest (SSSI) and the southern third is a National Nature Reserve managed by English Nature (formerly Nature Conservancy Council). A golf course covers part of the northern dunes, and Saunton Beach is surely one of the finest in Britain, a particularly safe shallow beach at its northern end, but perhaps less exciting and without the bigger waves of Putsborough and Croyde beaches to the north. Surfing has gone on for many years; we still have HW's own wooden board with his own symbol and initials scribed into it. But today all-weather wetsuits mean much more activity, whilst water-skiing and power-boating are prevalent.

In winter the swollen river waters of Taw and Torridge bring flotsam of oak and alder leaves, twigs and branches from waterside trees. The bodies of washed-up large jelly fish, once extremely common until the 1940s, and the sight of porpoises, and grey seals have now become very much more rare. One of HW's early stories concerned an almost mythical beast known locally as 'The Crake' (see *Tales of Moorland and Estuary*). This was Orca Gladiator, the killer whale, and the name used to conjure up terror, long before '*Jaws*' films were thought of!

The River Caen cuts northwards defining Braunton Marshes and Braunton Great Field (which HW called 'The Great Plain') from Chivenor Airfield on the far side, up to and beyond the town of Braunton, a place with many HW associations, not least The 'Ag' Inn, a favourite watering place.

On the far side of the Caen, opposite Marstage Farm, is Ramshorn Pond, where Tarka is finally parted from his mother and becomes an independent adult otter.

And so the route continues round the estuary back towards Barnstaple, wild and beautiful whether the tide is in or out.

Readers may like to know of the existence of The Henry Williamson Society set up in 1980 to encourage by all appropriate means, a wider readership and deeper understanding of the literary heritage left by the major twentieth century writer, Henry Williamson (1895-1977). For further details and a membership form please write to: P.F. Murphy, Esq., Membership Secretary, 16 Doran Drive, Redhill, Surrey, RH1 6AX.

MAPS AND ROUTE DETAILS

SECTION 9 BRAUNTON BURROWS AND THE ESTUARY
BRAUNTON BURROWS TO BARNSTAPLE
19 kilometres (12 miles)

MAP 30, 31, 32 + 33A, B, C

Join the main road for 300m (330 yds) to Saunton taking the first right turn beyond the entrance to the golf course. After about 100m (90 yds) turn right through a wooden gate, follow the signpost across the field and through another bridle gate where you turn left.

The route now takes you across the golf course and past Braunton Burrows a sand dune system managed as a National Nature Reserve. Walk along the sandy bridleway passing a barn and carry on in a southerly direction. As the track peters out bear left to go around the green in front, then continue south along the winding path. At the English Nature sign for the Burrows check the Ministry of Defence range notice and if there is no red flag flying continue until you reach a stone track. Turn left along this to come to the car park and turn right to follow the pot-holed road that takes you parallel to the coast. When the estuary comes into view the route forks left and follows a wide track behind the dunes that takes you past another car park and on to White House. At White House the path turns right, then left to continue along the top of a dyke for about 4km (2½ miles) and stays on this all the way into Braunton. On the way you pass Ram's Horn Pond where Tarka spent time when '. . . the Icicle Spirit gripped the land . . .'.

When the riverside walk finishes join the road and follow this till you come to a former level crossing. The route turns right along the former railway line for about 10km (6 miles) to Barnstaple. Turning left along the former railway line takes you to Braunton with its Tourist Information Centre, Countryside Centre, shops and services. As you approach Barnstaple, bear away from the river to pass behind the rugby ground grandstand following a track past the agricultural suppliers depot. Turn right across the front of the County Council depot and then immediately right again to follow the lane that takes you to Rolle Quay. Walk along here to the main road and cross the Rolle Bridge turning right to walk alongside the River Yeo. Follow the road round past the Civic Centre and walk across the car park here to join the Riverside Walk. Turn left along this and follow it to Barnstaple Long Bridge.

Braunton Burrows in winter (photo John Breeds)

MAP 30

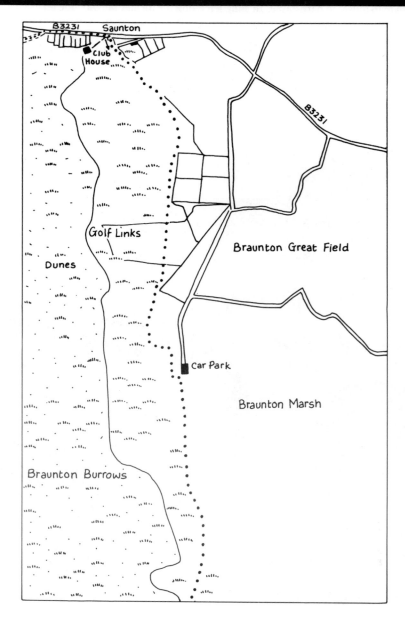

Section 9: Braunton Burrows and the Estuary, Saunton to Crow Point

MAP 31

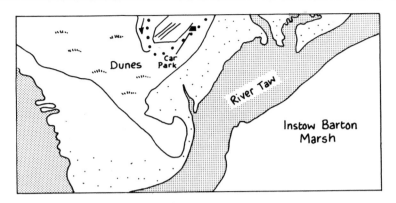

Section 9: Braunton Burrows and the Estuary, Crow Point

Cycleway

MAP 32

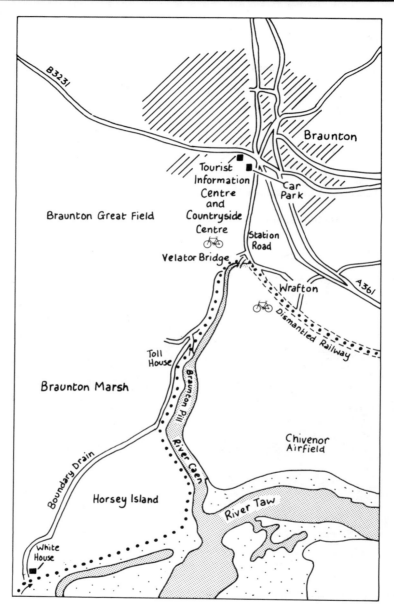

Section 9: Braunton Burrows and the Estuary, White House to Wrafton

MAP 33 A, B and C

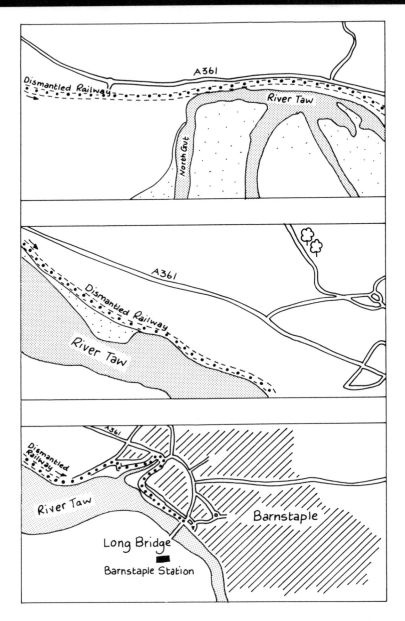

Section 9: Braunton Burrows and the Estuary, Wrafton to Barnstaple

NOTES